Inquiring

Safely

A Guide for
Middle School
Teachers

By Terry Kwan and Juliana Texley
With John Summers, Contributing Editor

NATIONAL SCIENCE TEACHERS ASSOCIATION
Arlington, Virginia

NSTApress
NATIONAL SCIENCE TEACHERS ASSOCIATION

Claire Reinburg, Director
J. Andrew Cocke, Associate Editor
Judy Cusick, Associate Editor
Betty Smith, Associate Editor

ART AND DESIGN Linda Olliver, Director
    Shennon Bersani, Cover art
    Linda Olliver, Interior illustration
PRINTING AND PRODUCTION Catherine Lorrain-Hale, Director
    Nguyet Tran, Assistant Production Manger
    Jack Parker, Desktop Publishing Specialist
MARKETING Holly Hemphill, Director
NSTA WEB Tim Weber, Webmaster
PERIODICALS PUBLISHING Shelley Carey, Director
sciLINKS Tyson Brown, Manager
    David Anderson, Web and Development Coordinator

NATIONAL SCIENCE TEACHERS ASSOCIATION
Gerald F. Wheeler, Executive Director
David Beacom, Publisher

Inquiring Safely: A Guide for Middle School Teachers
NSTA Stock Number: PB166X2
Printed in the USA by Kirby Lithographic Co., Inc. Printed on recycled paper.
05 04 03   4 3 2 1

Copyright © 2003 by the National Science Teachers Association

Library of Congress Cataloging-in-Publication Data
Kwan, Terry.
Inquiring safely : a guide for middle school teachers / by Terry Kwan
and Juliana Texley.
    p. cm.
Includes bibliographical references and index.
ISBN 0-87355-201-6 (pbk.)
1. Science—Study and teaching (Middle school) 2. Science rooms and
equipment—Safety measures. 3. Laboratories—Safety measures.
I. Texley, Juliana. II. Title.
Q181.K885 2003
507'.1'2—dc21   2002156186

Permission is granted in advance for reproduction for purpose of classroom or workshop instruction. To request permission for other uses, send specific requests to: NSTA Press, 1840 Wilson Boulevard, Arlington, Virginia 22201-3000. Website: *www.nsta.org*

Featuring SciLinks®—a new way of connecting text and the Internet. Up-to-the minute online content, classroom ideas, and other materials are just a click away. Go to page ix to learn more about this new educational resource.

Contents

Preface

Before last year's publication of *Exploring Safely: A Guide for Elementary Teachers*, it had been many years since the National Science Teachers Association had released a laboratory safety guide for teachers. In that time, many things have changed. We have more to teach, and the concepts are more complex. Technology has permitted us to gather and transmit information with increasing speed. We have access to new research and data about toxicity of materials and dangers in methods that were not apparent years ago. Social conditions have changed too. Today's teachers work with increasingly diverse student populations, including many students with special needs and sensitivities for whom they must design lab and field work. High-stakes tests have narrowed our focus and sharpened the scrutiny of our communities. The public is more litigious, increasing teachers' concerns about liability.

But today's students need hands-on experience in science more than ever. They need to observe and investigate, practicing the skills which will enable them to make good decisions and to work in the complex world of the twenty-first century.

The good news is that we now have information about alternatives and options that we never had before. We can still provide the investigative and observational activities that are essential to helping students understand the content and the methods of science. We can still set the scene for the discrete events that produce the "Aha!" so essential to engendering true understanding and love of the scientific endeavor.

Teachers today can implement exciting curricula based on the National Science Education Standards in a safe learning environment if they have background knowledge and good sense. To do so requires planning and preparation, but it's well worth the effort.

This book is the second in a series of three intended to offer positive options as they raise awareness of potential hazards. *Inquiring Safely* is the guide for middle school teachers. *Exploring Safely*, published last year, is for elementary school teachers, and *Investigating Safely* will be for high school teachers. We've included many anecdotes to highlight and reinforce ideas. Although we have changed the names and made some other modifications, all the stories are based on actual events.

The traditional safety manual tends to be a compilation of safety rules, regulations, and lists, but this book takes another path. We offer a more narrative style, providing discussions of safety concepts in the context of commonplace situations in real classrooms. We hope this approach makes these books enjoyable to read as well as to reference. Because we recognize that another way to use the book is to look for specific topics, we have included a detailed index to help you locate the information you need. You will also find that some of the same information is repeated in several sections. This is done to minimize flipping back and forth to find the information you need.

We hope the books are thought-provoking. No single publication can cover every eventuality or all the specific policies and rules promulgated by federal, state, and local authorities. There could never be a definitive list of *everything* that is unsafe, or a list of activities that would *always* be safe. We encourage you to make connections and generalize from the ideas presented, using informed common sense. Our goal is to provide you, the teacher, with examples of safe practices and to help you become more alert to ways of ensuring safety when you teach science in your classroom and in field studies. Above all, we encourage you to use common sense and stay up to date with best practice, state law, and district policies.

We believe creating a safe environment for teaching and learning science is a group endeavor, led by the teacher, but joined by the entire school community. As you read this book, we hope it helps you see your physical environment and your procedures through a safety-conscious lens. In so doing, you will be able to give your students habits of mind that will last a lifetime.

Acknowledgments

Thanks to Betty Smith, our editor at NSTA, and to the contributors who reviewed and added to this document: Sandra West, James Kaufman, Maxine Rosenberg, Kalle Gerritz, Sue Senator, Karen Byers, Andrew Braun, Richard Staley, Donald Korb, O.D., and Gloria Rudisch, M.D. Their tireless work has helped us polish our view of the classroom and enrich our offerings to you, the teacher. Special thanks to Robert E. Kilburn, longtime mentor and friend to author Terry Kwan.

The authors and contributing editor John Summers have been working together for many years as part of the NSTA TAPESTRY grant program funded by Toyota Motor Sales, U.S.A., Inc., and wish to acknowledge with thanks the generous support Toyota has provided to hundreds of science educators and thousands of their students for more than a decade.

Author Biographies

Terry Kwan taught middle school science before becoming a science supervisor and teacher trainer. For the past 15 years, she has been an independent contractor, collaborating with private and public institutions to develop science programs, train teachers, and design science facilities. She has been a school board member in Brookline, Massachusetts, since 1985 and a community representative to Institutional Biosafety Committees for the Harvard Medical School and the Dana Farber Cancer Institute.

Juliana Texley has taught all the sciences, K to 12, for 25 years and spent nine as a school superintendent. She was editor of *The Science Teacher* for 12 years and an officer of the Association of Presidential Awardees in Science Teaching. She currently teaches college biology and technology and develops online curricula for students and teachers.

About the Contributing Editor

John Summers has taught environmental sciences, biology, and chemistry for many years and continues to be actively involved in programs to support teaching and learning of the sciences at the precollege level. A presenter at numerous NSTA and American Association for the Advancement of Science conferences, he is also mentor to Toyota TAPESTRY grant winners and serves on panels to structure and review frameworks, assessments, and systemic initiatives in the state of Washington. His special interests include using science-oriented outdoor experiences to challenge and connect with at-risk students.

How can you and your students avoid searching hundreds of science websites to locate the best sources of information on a given topic? SciLinks, created and maintained by the National Science Teachers Association (NSTA), has the answer.

In a SciLinked text, such as this one, you'll find a logo and keyword near a concept your class is studying, a URL (*www.scilinks.org*), and a keyword code. Simply go to the SciLinks website, type in the code, and receive an annotated listing of as many as 15 Web pages—all of which have gone through an extensive review process conducted by a team of science educators. SciLinks is your best source of pertinent, trustworthy Internet links on subjects from astronomy to zoology.

Need more information? Take a tour—http://www.scilinks.org/tour/

Setting the Scene

Basic Rules for a Safer Science Classroom

Six classes, six teachers—just navigating middle school is a voyage of discovery for early adolescents. We offer them a confusing array of choices, many in science. Sometimes it seems we spend too much science class time teaching organization, caution, and control. But these skills—critical to making science experiences exciting and safe—are also important science processes.

Middle School—Home of the Brave

Unbounded exuberance, unchecked enthusiasm, limitless energy, daring spirit—students with the curiosity and emerging reasoning skills that are "the right stuff" for an investigative science program come into middle schools. Early adolescents are exploring their expanded world in new and strange vehicles—growing bodies they have yet to understand, much less control. These years offer wonderful opportunities to capture students' energy and channel it toward the excitement of scientific exploration. But everything we do in our middle school science classrooms must recognize the developmental level of our young scientists and their penchant for risk-taking that we must temper sufficiently to promote safety.

Share the Adventure *and* the Responsibility

An investigative science program requires the distribution, use, and care of much more material and equipment than a textbook/workbook program. Learning through doing engages middle school students, but you and your students need to share ownership of the process to make it successful. The students must join in the responsibility for tracking myriad items and cleaning up the inevitable messes associated with laboratory science. Most middle school students, left to their own devices, do not remember to do things like returning equipment to the correct storage place, washing first and cleaning before leaving the room, or using the safety goggles you told them about just yesterday. It is not that they are unwilling to help; it is that competing priorities make it easy to forget. So, if you are to enjoy a safe investigative venture together, you must specifically plan to make your students full partners in managing the laboratory environment.

The Schedule's the Thing

Ideally, science teachers should be assigned their own rooms and have no more than two preparations a day. If science rooms must be shared, they should be shared only with other science teachers. The potential hazards, and the value, of materials and equipment in a science room make its use by a nonscience specialist potentially dangerous. If your principal is unaware of the safety risks associated with using science facilities for nonscience classes, you may need to point them out.

Notes to Administrators: Scheduling a Safer Science Program

▶ Assign science rooms only to science teachers.
▶ Avoid assigning more than one teacher to each science room.
▶ Avoid assigning science teachers to more than one room.
▶ Provide prep periods in the science room as part of the teacher's schedule between different assignments.
▶ Provide secure locked storage for prepared science materials.

Moving a science teacher from one room to another for different class periods should also be discouraged. A laboratory science program requires access to materials and equipment and time for preparing them. Ideally, equipment should be stored in appropriate secure facilities at the point of use. Doing this is very difficult if you must move from room to room or switch from one science subdiscipline to another. For optimum safety, time for preparation should be part of the teacher's schedule, and different classes should be separated by a prep.

The Teachable Moment

Many textbooks begin with a general chapter on safety. Although this may be prudent, it doesn't mean much to students if the chapter is abstract and isolated. As with everything else, safety lessons are best remembered when they are associated with real experiences. Although you may want to review and post some general safety rules — hand-washing rules, use of safety glasses—right from the start, the best time to give specific safety instruction is in conjunction with a lesson or activity when the safety procedure is needed. Even though the procedure is one you may have reviewed a number of times, go over it again every time the activity you have planned requires the precaution.

Following the introduction of a new safety procedure, you might have students create signs and posters. This reinforces the point and makes a good authentic assessment. Assign students to place safety reminder signs near the activities that call for reminders. For example, put hand-washing signs near live animal cages and safety goggles reminders near areas where chemicals are used. You will know students have mastered safety concepts when they can explain them to visitors, new students, and returning absentees.

Less Is Better

Although we know an active investigative science program requires lively discussion and movement, some teachers mistakenly believe noisy, bustling students are an indication of successful hands-on, minds-on science. Not only is this untrue, but such activity also may work against your program. Think of your science program as interesting, fascinating, and challenging rather than fun. Learn to distinguish the considerable difference between intense discussion and just plain noise. Moving about to collect supplies and make observations looks and sounds different than jostling, shuffling, and hanging out.

Less is better—less noise, less material, less movement. Carefully storing supplies and materials in a safer, more organized fashion is not the same as accumulating junk. You create a safer environment when you reduce the supplies, the talk, and the movement to only what is necessary.

Tell students to leave outerwear, unneeded books, notebooks, backpacks, and other treasures in their lockers or in a storage area away from the lab work areas. If items are hung over the backs of the students' chairs, the extra weight can cause the chairs to tip over when the student stands up or pushes the chair away from the table. Refer to clothing instructions in Chapter 10 ("Dress of the Day," p. 135). Food and food containers should never be anywhere near the spaces intended for science experiments.

The Best-Laid Plans

Middle school students need structure, direction, and clear expectations. Detailed planning is essential and so are communicating expectations and setting limits. Make sure every lesson has a beginning, a middle, and an end. Give directions and goals before anyone begins work. Specify the safety issues and procedures even if you are repeating an instruction. Make sure everyone stops working when it is time to clean up, return equipment, and decontaminate work areas. No one should leave until everyone is checked out.

Saving Moments

- Save unused plastic cups, old cafeteria trays, and clean trays from prepackaged foods for distributing materials. Once used for labs, don't use these items for any other purpose.
- Keep supplies in a locked area.
- Measure out needed supplies in advance. Keep stock bottles locked up during class.
- Establish a regular system for distributing and collecting materials and supplies; train students to participate.
- If you must move materials and supplies, move only small quantities in locked storage units.
- When equipment is limited, alternate lab days for half the class with desk or computer workstation activities such as investigation planning, data analysis, and data graphing for the other half.
- Post safety instructions on an overhead transparency or in a computer database for review.

Whether you are a new teacher or a veteran, if you establish the discipline of preparing complete and detailed plans, you will lower your stress and your liability. As you'll see in Chapter 11 ("The Best Defense," p. 152), these plans not only create peace of mind but also are valuable documentation in case a problem ever occurs.

But remember that detailed lesson plans can look great on paper but fall short in practice. The best format is easy for you to follow and complete in a reasonable amount of time. You might create columns in your plan book to list materials to purchase, time requirements, chemical allocations, and safety reminders.

Providing students with a written version of your instructions and safety directions and repeating them at the beginning of each class is important. If at all possible, avoid students' leaving your class when you give directions. A student who reenters the room in the middle of a science experience can be a hazard to the rest of the group. When students are absent, they may miss safety directions. Keep an explicit record of what safety instruction has been given, when, and to which students. Keep this checklist as evidence that you gave proper and appropriate safety information to each student.

Your planning also must consider the consequences of both teacher and student absences. Every day there is someone absent in almost every classroom.

Remember you are responsible for the program offered by your substitute. Because your substitute is unlikely to have your knowledge of the subject matter or your control of the classroom, it is best to have a substitute conduct nonlaboratory activities or those without potential hazards. If you direct a substitute to do an activity that results in an accident, you could be held liable. (See Chapter 11, "Substitute Teachers, Interns, and Student Teachers," p. 149.) If you will be absent for an extended period, request a science-trained substitute.

Many teachers prepare a special substitute folder for unexpected one-day absences. This folder contains instructions for nonlaboratory science activities that fit almost any part of the year. Take time to speak to your substitutes and ensure they are competent to carry out your plans. Your students can assume a great deal of responsibility when you are away if they are accustomed to sharing the routine of your classroom.

Students who are absent need to make up lab activities. They must have access to supplies and missed instructions and must do these activities under your direct supervision—never in a hall or storeroom. To make the process easier, organize materials in labeled boxes or bins containing the supplies and instructions for a particular activity or unit. Place a laminated card with the relevant safety rules in with the supplies. Although clear or translucent containers are ideal, shoeboxes and the 10-ream copy paper cartons may also serve you well. Create outside labels that not only show the title of the activity but also list the items inside. (See Chapter 4, p. 37, for storage tips.)

Many teachers find assigning students homework buddies or makeup-work buddies a helpful practice. Teach cooperation and responsibility along with science, especially if you have heterogeneous classes and special needs students. Every student should feel responsible for every other member of his or her science team every day.

For Whom the Bell Tolls

When planning science activities, make sure you account for set-up and clean-up time within the lesson. Distributing materials at the beginning of the class, collecting materials at the end, and cleaning up the work space and used equipment take real time to do properly. Your students should see this as part of their responsibility. Because these housekeeping tasks are an integral part of the entire science activity, make sure you build your schedule with enough time to complete them. If you have set up a specific time to do a science activity, then make sure no one begins before everything is properly distributed and everyone has stopped the activity when it is time to clean up.

See that work surfaces are washed and dried completely after any science activity before going on to the next. This is a great habit to instill even if it sometimes doesn't seem necessary. Make cleanup a responsibility for students, but have them use only mild dish detergent. You will need a material safety data sheet (MSDS) for the cleaners. (See Chapter 4, p. 41, for more information.) Do not allow students to leave the room for appointments or pullout programs unless they first clean up their work areas.

Building in "think time" is also important. When students do a lab or other hands-on activity and then run out the door before they analyze what happened and why, they may not get much benefit. That sometimes means preplanning to break lab experiences into smaller lessons, with discussion, journal, and cleanup time built in rather than trying to squeeze everything into a single period. If your lesson feels rushed, it probably is. Redesign the activity, expand it to multiple periods, use self-reflections as homework, or find an alternative that permits you and your class enough time to think about the activity, not just complete it.

> ## Making Every Minute Count
>
> ### A Typical Lesson
> ▶ Overview and safety tips (5 minutes)
> ▶ Distribution of supplies (5 minutes)
> ▶ Activity period (10 minutes)
> ▶ Assessment break (5 minutes)
> ▶ Activity continues (10 minutes)
> ▶ Cleanup and equipment check (10 minutes)
> ▶ Brief review and prep for followup and/or homework (5 minutes)
> Total_____ (50 minutes)

Homework Happens

You are responsible and can be held liable for assignments you give as homework. Therefore, consider assignments carefully. Do not ask students to explore chemicals in their home cabinets without adult supervision or test soils from unknown grounds. On the other hand, don't hesitate to develop safer home assignments for students to share with parents. Many teachers have created portable science kits—backpacks or boxes—that students can check out. They contain such things as measuring tools, binoculars and star charts, or leaf presses. Parents, facing the growing independence of their preteens, appreciate structured opportunities for interaction. Once families have explored together, they are more likely to continue to do so.

Many of the safety practices you promote in science activities can be extended easily to students' homes. Reading labels carefully, the proper handling of sharp instruments and glassware, hand washing and cleanup—all have practical applications in the typical kitchen or bathroom. When you give instructions to keep students safer during field studies, these same rules may help keep them safer when traveling with their parents. So take the opportunity, and invite your students to think of how a rule you have just taught them would apply equally well to a situation at home. Help students to think safety wherever they are and whatever they are doing. Because middle schoolers gradually become more reluctant to discuss school at home, you may want to create an assignment that requires this sort of communication. Parents will welcome the chance for interaction.

If you have a newsletter, voice mail on your school phone, a website, or send out e-mail to parents, you might create a changing message: "This week's lesson encourages hand washing …" or "Parents, check your students' journals for safety rules concerning the handling of …" Encourage students to work with parents to create a child-safe home, especially if younger siblings are present.

Say It Again, Sam

Making Connections

- phone calls
- newsletters
- homework assignments and hotlines
- progress reports
- e-mail
- websites

Repetition is the key to success with middle school students, who may be highly logical in some ways but quite concrete in others. Middle school students are often willing to tutor elementary students on safety, showing off their new maturity to their former schoolmates. Every new application of the ideas you present will help reinforce safety and make it a habit.

If your school has an Internet connection or a homework hotline, make sure safety concepts are included. Many teachers develop safety rules agreements with their students and have parents review them at home early in the year. It's a good idea to update and repeat the contract process each quarter.

Midden Heap or Laboratory?

The physical environment can enhance or detract from your lessons. In middle school, keeping the learning space neat, attractive, and safe can be quite a challenge, because classrooms are no longer self-contained and there is lots of movement in and out. Sometimes it feels like no one owns the space. But when maintaining the learning space is the shared responsibility of everyone who uses it—teachers and students alike—the problem becomes more manageable. As teacher, you are the model; your students will keep their work space clean and neat only if you keep the rest of the classroom that way.

Clutter creates tripping hazards and blocks fire exits. Easily distracted students become more so in messy environments. Most important, a messy, junk-filled room detracts from the impression of a classroom/laboratory as a place for serious business.

Reduce the amount of materials you accumulate. Paper is combustible. Check local fire regulations to ensure that the amount of paper on walls and ceilings conforms to the fire code. Mobiles and hanging paper can be fire hazards.

Be rigorous about throwing things out. Avoid the pack rat syndrome. Anything you have not used in two years, you are not likely to use ever again. You need only one good copy of that favorite lesson, and you might consider saving documents and plans on a CD-ROM. (See Chapter 3 for more tips about facilities and Chapter 4 for more on storage.)

You do not have to be an artist or spend precious dollars on elaborate posters for bulletin and trim boards. Student work and data from lab activities make the best displays of all. Students who stare at the walls can learn from what surrounds them in their classrooms. Use your board space to display student work that emphasizes continuing themes and ongoing safety rules. Put a safety theme on a bulletin board and encourage students to bring in photos to illustrate it. Make a feature out of the classroom fire escape route and emergency instructions. Encourage students to develop posters reminding one another of hand washing, proper disposal, and recycling.

A Reputation for Excellence

Science is highly motivating. For that reason, a good science teacher can become something of a local hero in the middle school. But it is critical for you to understand that excellence does not mean doing high school science at the middle school level. Students in grades 5 through 8 have content and process needs and developmental maturity different than high schoolers'. Trying to transpose that great lab from high school to middle school, even if it generates excitement or enthusiasm, is not a good idea. Such a practice may make good press but is usually not good education and may create serious safety hazards.

Because middle school students move around the school more than they did in elementary grades, corridor and other common-area displays can call attention to the work going on in your science program and attract students to your science place—a classroom with mini-museums, displays, and interactive bulletin boards. But becoming the local gathering place has its complications. The rules for safety must be clear enough that even the casual visitor will learn them quickly. Be especially careful if you maintain live organisms in your classroom or mini-museum. You are responsible for the safety of visitors and organisms and must ensure against mischief. Make sure your room is supervised or locked during change of class.

Make all your students docents in your classroom. Give them a sense of ownership, and encourage them to explain the rules—and why they are necessary—to visitors. You may want to set up a few test runs with some invited guests so you can test the students for both hospitality and safety consciousness.

Students can share the excitement of their lessons via the computer. Middle school students can produce PowerPoint slides of their experiments that can be scrolled at a workstation in the media center or in your room during parent night. Middle schoolers have created great Web pages for their school sites. An inexpensive digital camera can be used to prepare displays allowing you and your students to share their science experiences without having constant traffic in the room.

Remember, it is far better to have a reputation for inquiry than for chaos. If people who enter your room find they are challenged to think, you'll become that local hero.

Set High Expectations

As any veteran teacher knows, high achievement is the reward for setting high expectations for our students. This is as true for safety as for any other expectation. The more you make students responsible for using and enforcing safe laboratory and fieldwork procedures, the more easily safe practice can become habit. Once you have established a classroom climate based on the expectation that students should be as vigilant as you in spotting safety hazards and eliminating them, you may find that fewer rules can work better than rules for every step and procedure. Middle school students respond well to greater responsibilities. "Now that you are older" almost guarantees cooperation. Your students are your best tools for a safe science environment. The ultimate safety rule should be: "Don't do anything you know or think might be unsafe for yourself or others."

With an inquiry-based science program, you are likely to encourage students to experiment, observe, and explore on their own in addition to following your step-by-step instructions. But there can be no experimentation with safety rules. When it comes to safety instructions and safe procedures, you must be explicit and exacting—especially with your middle school students who are so often distracted by their other interests. Although safe practices support inquiry-based science, do not let students learn by trial and error when it comes to matters of safety. If you catch your students quoting you, you've succeeded.

THE SAVVY SCIENCE TEACHER

Ms. B's classroom was becoming quite a zoo. Newly born animals were generating so much interest and excitement that the room was constantly filled with visiting students running in to check on the broods. During one change of class, a young animal was almost crushed between a wheel and the wall of the cage by an overly enthusiastic visitor. Something had to be done.

Ms. B went to the school's technology teacher for help and found a solution. Now, each day, her students take a 25-second MPEG video of the latest developments in the gerbil habitat and narrate it for the school's closed circuit television broadcast. The report has become a highlight of the daily program. Next month, other classes plan to join Ms. B's team in reporting on their study of a local stream.

Connections
- American Chemical Society. 2001. *Safety in the Elementary (K–6) Science Classroom* (2nd ed.). Washington, D.C. American Chemical Society.
- NSTA Press. 2003. *Safety in the Elementary Classroom.* Arlington, VA: NSTA Press.

Communities of Learners

Promoting Safety for Every Student

> In elementary school, teachers meet each spring to carefully evaluate students and create heterogeneous classes. But in middle school, class assignments may be done by a computer program influenced more by the need to schedule activities such as band and football than by planning for balanced distribution. The characteristics of any one section may be radically different from others. The same lesson planned for the first-period class may need a complete overhaul to accommodate the students in the fifth period. Each class is different, and the accommodations you make for safety should be consistent with the specific needs of the students in the class.

Science for All

One pervasive theme in the *National Science Education Standards* (NRC 1996) is that our goals are meant for all students—regardless of learning style, background, or ability. Supporting all learners becomes more difficult in middle school for two reasons: Students exhibit greater differences in achievement and skill at the same time that subject matter requirements are more rigid, and they are more reluctant to communicate their needs to parents or teachers.

But middle school teachers may have some advantages over their elementary and high school counterparts. The ideal middle school team enjoys joint planning time for three or four teachers of different disciplines, giving them the option of planning interdisciplinary activities. If this is your situation, take advantage of the opportunity to see different dimensions of your students and get insights and tips for managing a student who may be difficult for you but a star with one of your colleagues. If your school does not specifically schedule joint planning time, you can arrange it informally. The benefits make the extra effort well worth it, and safety can be a part of the team effort.

Other sources of support for diverse learners are guidance counselors, school psychologists, special education and learning disability specialists, school nurses, aides, and other paraprofessionals. Remember also that your subject, taught with a hands-on investigative approach, holds its own fascination and brings success within reach of a wide range of students. Set a goal of having every student succeed safely.

Topic: learners with disabilities
Go to: www.scilinks.org
Code: SML12

Least Restrictive Environments

Public Law 94–142, also known as the Individuals with Disabilities Education Act (IDEA), a federal law passed in 1975 and reauthorized in 1990 and 1997, mandates that all children receive a free and appropriate public education regardless of the level or severity of their disabilities. IDEA requires that, to the greatest extent possible, students with disabilities be educated with students who do not have disabilities. The law states that "unless a child's individualized education program requires some other arrangement, the child is (to be) educated in the school which he or she would attend if not disabled [Section 121a.522(c)]." It requires that removal of the child from the regular classroom occur only when education in regular classes "with the use of supplementary aids and services cannot be achieved satisfactorily [Section 121a.550(2)]." This means that, if it is possible and practical for a student to learn a subject in a regular education classroom, it must happen that way.

Subsequent rules stipulate a student may not be disciplined if the behavior causing the discipline results from a disability. This provision often confuses and complicates middle school management. It's important to be aware of the behavioral limitations documented for your students and plan accordingly. But these rules don't mean you have to tolerate unsafe behavior. They mean you may need to make a special effort to define the rules, set up shorter free periods, or limit access to certain types of supplies. They may require a discussion of behavior in advance or specific assignments in cooperative groups. They also may mean that certain lab experiences are simply not appropriate for certain groups of students. Don't be trapped by the illusion that the high-risk experiences are invaluable at this age—replacing them with simpler explorations, using smaller quantities of chemicals or less risky procedures will give everyone more time to relax and learn.

Even if your classes contain no identified special needs students with physical or behavioral disabilities, you should recognize that, for some students and some classes, the "chemistry" is just not right. A lab activity that is perfectly reasonable for your first period class may be highly risky for another group. Use your experience, professional judgment, and good common sense to modify or omit certain lab experiences to fit the group and the circumstances.

Learning together is almost always possible for even the most diverse group of middle school students. But to encourage safety, you may need to modify your procedures or insist on extra help. Participate in the individual education plan (IEP) conference for each of your special needs students, and come prepared with information that describes the equipment, facilities modifications, and other accommodations you will need to allow the student to participate fully in your class activities. For example, if your normal procedure requires completing a written pretest on safety prior to a lab, ask your clinician to help with individualized testing to ensure that the learning-disabled student understands fully. If there are certain labs that could pose a high risk with behaviorally challenged students, list the risks and request assistance from a co-teacher or paraprofessional. Don't forget you will have to spend time for planning and preparing the support personnel. (See Chapter 11, "A Diversity of Needs," p. 148.)

The Americans with Disabilities Act (ADA) of 1990 (*http://www.usdoj.gov/crt/ada/pubs/ada.txt*) prohibits discrimination against persons with disabilities. Like IDEA, this act mandates open access to regular educational facilities for people who are disabled. But ADA goes beyond special education. Where IDEA guides us in educating students working below their abilities, ADA guides us in providing access to our facilities and programs for all members of the community—teachers, students, parents, and members of the general public. Complying with ADA is a general education function and often includes measures that must be taken by regular education teachers. But it also requires the full cooperation of the administration. If a physically disabled student is assigned to your room, you should know all the details in advance. It is the school's responsibility to ensure you have all the equipment you need. That may mean different furnishings (see "An ADA Checklist"), Braille, text on tape, sound amplification equipment, earphones, personal word processors, or other assistive devices.

An ADA Checklist

▶ 86 cm aisles for wheelchairs with appropriate turning radii
▶ 70 cm of knee space
▶ A sink no higher than 86 cm and no deeper than 17 cm with paddle handles
▶ Paddle handles at sinks and on doors
▶ All entrances wider than 86 cm
▶ All flooring leveled or ramped
▶ A clear emergency exit through accessible doorways (avoid routes through automatic fire doors)
▶ Clear sight lines from a sitting position
▶ Locked storage
▶ No protruding cabinets
▶ Access to the safety shower
▶ Braille labels on safety equipment

Every state has its own regulations for IDEA and ADA. Many of these regulations are more detailed than the federal laws, but all are based in the same philosophy and goals: to remove barriers and support achievement. Our communities of learners should be open to everyone. It's up to you to determine how this can be achieved in your curriculum and incumbent on you to request the support needed to make the student's experience successful.

A Special Set of Eyes

It takes a special set of eyes and ears to make sure our classrooms don't present barriers to any budding scientist. Many professional preparation programs help by requiring prospective teachers to spend time in a wheelchair, on crutches, or with muffled vision or hearing. The experience usually gives the teacher a very different perspective. The suggestions in this chapter do not cover every possible barrier, but they can provide your school team with a place to start.

Begin your observations by looking at the physical facilities in which you teach science. Remember that middle school students are gangly and growing. Your facilities must be scaled to suit. To accommodate a physically disabled student, you will need even more space—probably twice as much—and specialized equipment. A wheelchair may be as wide as 86 cm and may take up even more room if the wheels are cambered, or tilted out, for a paraplegic. Wall-mounted objects should not be higher than 86 cm from the floor, and there should be at least 70 cm of knee space under the desks. Many disabled persons must sit on special cushions to prevent pressure sores. This increases knee space requirements. Sinks must not be more than 17 cm deep and must have paddle handles for persons for whom turning knobs would be a problem.

The floor must be flat, including the path to the safety shower, and there should be no barriers such as taped-down wires or uneven carpet-tile interfaces. Make sure there is a good clear exit path from the room in case of fire. Don't rely on a route through a fire door that may close automatically if the fire alarm sounds.

Think about visually impaired students as you inspect your room. You may need Braille labels. Wall-mounted units should be placed above base cabinets. There should be no protruding edges or corners on casework and furnishings, an accommodation for visually impaired students that is valuable for everyone. You should also be conscious that acids, glues, or solvents can make fingertips lose their sensitivity, a problem for students who read Braille.

In designing a new facility, architects should be familiar with the requirements of ADA and should incorporate them into the plan. If you teach in an older facility, you may be "grandfathered," exempt from ADA requirements until you remodel. But you won't have any grace period under IDEA. You must create an immediate plan for changes when a disabled or special education student needs access. So, until a major remodeling project occurs, you would probably need to add portable lab stations, adjustable-height tables, and alternative sink stations.

Listen Up

Hearing loss can be a condition from birth, acquired from infections or allergies, or the result of damage from severe or prolonged sound exposure. The loss can be slight to severe. A hearing loss can result in subtle but serious barriers to learning, because it may prevent a student's comprehending spoken language. Hearing problems can be exacerbated by classrooms with sound-absorbing high ceilings and carpeted floors. In a large middle school, constant background noise from human activity and air-handling equipment can make the problem even worse. This may explain why some students don't pay attention to your directions—they may not have heard them.

Many students have selected-frequency hearing loss. For example, students may confuse fricatives such as /s/, /f/, or /sh/. You may find that students with this type of hearing loss think they understood you when in fact they did not hear your words clearly and misinterpreted what you said. With hearing loss in specific frequencies, words and parts of words are lost, but the mind invents what might have been said. The result is that what the student understands is not what you said. This is different from and potentially far more serious than not hearing the instruction at all. Even normal-hearing middle school students are reluctant to admit they need help when they may not have heard your instruction. To deter these pitfalls, avoid simply asking students if they heard and understood your instructions. Instead, ask them to rephrase your instructions or apply what you just said.

Some schools have countered the hearing problem by installing sound-amplification systems. These systems may include the use of a small lavalier microphone on the teacher's lapel and speakers placed in the ceiling or walls. Some new school designs include headset microphones and classroom sound systems in science classrooms.

Sound amplification systems have an important safety value for you as a teacher too. Many years of extended abuse of the vocal cords—"teacher voice"—can gradually erode the tissues. Because there is no pain sensation in the vocal cords, the damage can occur without any clear signs. You may feel tired, your voice may crack, and you may find colds have a tendency to settle in the compromised tissues. Two kinds of damage can occur: polyps, which must be removed surgically, and erosion of the vocal cord tissue (*myasthenia laryngis*), which is incurable. As an employee, you have the right to reasonable assistance to avoid this problem. *Never* resort to generating a consistent, loud teacher voice. It's bad for you and doesn't help your students develop self-control or listening skills.

SIGNAL VS. NOISE

Increasing the loudness of speech does not necessarily make it more easily understood by the hard of hearing. Raising the S/N, the signal-to-noise ratio, can be more important than raising your voice. The signal is the sound the listener is attempting to hear or distinguish. The noise is the ambient noise in the room. For speech to be heard clearly, the S/N must be high: The sound to be heard must be loud as compared to other noise in the room, such as side conversations, ventilation fans whirring away, and machines humming. This is the idea behind the use of FM amplification systems. The teacher's speech is picked up by a microphone on the teacher's lapel and delivered amplified directly to the student's earpiece so, to the student, the teacher's voice sounds louder than the ambient noise.

Accommodating Learning Disabilities

Being able to read at grade level shouldn't be the entry test for learning science, although it often is. Consider these issues as you plan your science activities:

- Directions should be provided in a variety of verbal and nonverbal formats—especially needed for students who must make up work missed during absences due to illness or to attending pullout programs.

- Students with reading or writing disabilities need opportunities to demonstrate achievement by applying concepts in a nonverbal format.

- Learning-disabled students often have less patience for sequential procedures if the sequence is not clear.

- Some nonverbal learning-disabled students and students in the autism spectrum respond very well to clear sequential procedures. Mayer-Johnson symbolic instructions may be a good addition to written/verbal instructions. See *www.Mayer-Johnson.com* for more information.

Give directions orally as well as in writing, and be conscious of the reading level of your activity and instruction sheets. Put major directions on a chart board or an overhead transparency, and display them during the activity. Provide graphic and symbolic support for written instructions. Before a group begins its work, have students rate each other on understanding safety directions. Remember that peer and social pressure play large roles in middle school behavior. Your students may learn more from one another than from adult authorities. Consider using performance assessments for basic safety skills such as using droppers, transferring liquids and solids, and using measuring tools.

Atoms Aren't All That Jiggles

Heterogeneous classes almost always include students with behavior problems as well as those with physical and learning disabilities. Autism, fetal alcohol syndrome, and other disorders may decrease a student's ability to detect interpersonal cues and exercise normally expected judgment. Hormonal fluctuations in the normal pre-adolescent can also contribute to the diverse behavior exhibited by middle schoolers.

Even students who have no systemic handicaps can have short attention spans. Your students spend far more time in front of frenetically paced media than they spend in your classroom. But there is no way a science lab can be safe at the pace of MTV.

To minimize accidents and increase students' attention span, begin with small steps. Start with five-minute experiences. Encourage careful observation. Have students give feedback on each other's work. Have them repeat or rephrase directions one or more times. Plan breaks in activities that change focus or change pace.

Keep your classroom neat and organized, and give students some of the responsibility for maintaining order. Maximize the uncluttered space in student work areas, so a sudden move can't result in an overturned piece of furniture. This may mean giving away some furniture or boxing up some treasures you have kept just in case you need them. Set up your grading system to reward responsible self-control.

You may find that science holds a magic key to better attention and better performance in some behaviorally challenged students.

Tips for ADHD Students

- Keep experiences and activities short, including labs.
- Post directions and have students act out essential safety precautions.
- Carefully consider the composition of student groups.
- Don't keep a cluttered room. Put away everything unnecessary.
- Keep the room as quiet as possible. Encourage discussion, but discourage loud voices and random chatting.
- Plan a method to get students' attention without shouting—a special clap, a blinking light, or a sign. Practice it before you try it during laboratory work.
- Consider having students use assistive technologies such as word processors for taking notes.
- Give small leadership responsibilities to reward responsible behavior.

Attention Deficit Disorder (ADD)

Attention Deficit Disorder (ADD) may affect the behavior and performance of students without producing hyperactivity (ADHD). What seems inherent to the middle school nature—losing track of time, space, and matter—may be a problem bigger for some students than others. If you find students who seem to try hard to remember your instructions, get work done on time, and get their act together, but never seem to make it, consider the possibility that their neurons may be wired somewhat differently, and attention deficit disorder may be affecting their performance. In these cases, just trying harder may not be the answer. They may need a more thorough evaluation and specific assistance. Some techniques that help students with ADD may benefit all middle schoolers to some degree:

- Break up instructions into smaller one-task steps.

- Provide checklists that literally require placing a check mark on the sheet before proceeding to the next step.

- Structure activities so that all the members of a group or a specifically-assigned partner check each other's work at regular and timely intervals.

For more information, *Driven to Distraction,* by Edward Hallowell, M.D., and John J. Ratey, M.D. (Pantheon Books 1995), is a book that provides easily comprehensible descriptions of many of the signs and symptoms of ADD plus many practical tips.

Learning English

If your class includes students who are not native speakers of English, you should have safety signage that uses universally understood symbols and/or is in the languages of these students. You might enlist the help of parent groups to help label your class-room appropriately and translate important directions to other languages.

To Your Good Health

The preceding tips are designed to deal with long-term or permanent disabilities. But teachers must also accommodate, and take steps to minimize, problems caused by temporary impairments and illnesses.

The common cold is becoming more common in classrooms. With fewer parents at home full time, there is a growing tendency to send students to school sick. Teachers need to recognize the signs of communicable diseases such as scabies (a parasitic mite infection), conjunctivitis (pink eye), impetigo (a bacterial skin infection), ring worm (a fungal skin infection), and head lice (pediculosis) that are all too common in the school environment. In most cases, students with these illnesses must be excluded from classes. Students should be immunized against measles and chicken pox, but teachers should still be familiar with the appearance of those rashes. Learn what poison ivy/oak rashes and insect bites look like as well. You should refer student with any rashes to the school nurse or other designated school health professional.

Allergies may look like colds, but they persist and aren't infectious. But the hygiene rules for coughs and colds apply to allergy symptoms, because infections take advantage of allergy-inflamed tissues. Be aware of the possible presence of allergens in your room. Check student health records early in the year to familiarize yourself with students who have allergies, and make sure that things you keep around your classroom do not exacerbate allergies. See Chapter 5, p. 53, and Chapter 10, "Persistent Problems," p. 130, for more information about allergens. Remember that allergic reactions can become life-threatening conditions very quickly. If a student develops hives or any sign of respiratory distress, call for medical help immediately.

Make sure you are familiar with your state regulations and district policies on dispensing medications. Do not provide medication—prescription or over-the-counter—to any student unless you are trained and directed by a physician. Even the most common over-the-counter medication can cause a severe reaction. Never administer nonprescription medicine of any kind. You are not qualified, authorized, or insured to do so. Discourage the practice of students' bringing their own medications to school unless they are prescribed by a physician. If a student must have medication at school, it should be in an original prescription bottle

Fighting Infection

▶ Remind parents in newsletters and e-mail to keep sick students at home.

▶ Send students with visible signs of illness or infection to the office.

▶ Keep tissues handy and reinforce use and proper disposal.

▶ Keep soap near the sink to encourage hand washing by students and teachers alike.

▶ Ask that your room be kept relatively cool.

▶ Keep nonlatex gloves handy.

SCI*LINKS*.
THE WORLD'S A CLICK AWAY

Topic: infectious diseases
Go to: *www.scilinks.org*
Code: SML19

labeled with the student's name and physician directions. Medication should be administered in the office in the presence of a trained professional. Students should not store medication in their desks or lockers.

A SIDEBAR ON SIDE EFFECTS

Images and advertising in the media have led students to be very casual about drugs. Both prescription and over-the-counter medications are heavily advertised. Characters on television portray drug use as benign and inconsequential. Students also may hold the same misconception as many adults about medication dosage: If a little is good, then a lot is better. A student investigation of the powerful effects and side effects of common drugs can be a valuable research project. Up-to-date information can be obtained through the Internet, but you must be careful to preview and screen all Internet sources. (Refer to Chapter 10, "The Internet Connection," p. 137.)

One drug that merits special attention is Ritalin. Many students must take Ritalin during the school day. Fellow students may observe or know about this. There have been increasing incidents of Ritalin abuse and sale of pills on school campuses. Most students do not recognize Ritalin's serious side effects, particularly for individuals without ADHD.

A Little Help from Your Friends

Many schools are encouraging the use of co-teachers to support the inclusion of special needs students in the regular education classroom. These additional adults can be a tremendous help and a valued safety measure. But the regular teacher must take a great deal of responsibility to make the partnership work effectively.

Co-teachers may not have the preparation for teaching science the science teacher has, but they will have special skills in assessment, behavior modification, and remedial reading that can help special needs students succeed in science. Treat your co-teacher as a partner. Plan jointly, and alternate the role of lead teacher. It takes continuing in-depth conversation for a co-teaching relationship to work well.

When setting up a co-teaching classroom, be wary of opportunistic scheduling. When a co-teacher is assigned to a heterogeneous classroom, it is to support a specific special education student or students whose requirements are described in IEPs. But some schools add other students with mild to severe behavior problems to the same section just because two teachers are available. This is unfair to the special education students and to the teachers. There is a synergistic effect when too many students with behavioral difficulties are assigned to the same section. Heterogeneity means there should be a good mix in every section.

For a complex high-structure lab activity, consider requesting paraprofessional assistance. If you work with paraprofessionals, you must allocate planning time with them. Do not expect your paraprofessional to learn along with the students. Go over safety precautions—including all of the things that might happen—in advance and insist that paras be given paid time to learn the science methods they need.

Treasuring Diversity

A heterogeneous class has great value. The sensitivity students develop when they work in groups with students of differing abilities can't be overestimated. This sensitivity to the needs of others is especially important in middle school, where both social interaction and egocentric behavior are commonplace.

JOINING THE CIRCLE

The middle school years bring emotional volatility as well as strong circles of friendship. Some circles emerge as cliques exerting powerful peer pressure on those who are "in" and those who are "out." Limit-testing is often the price of admission. But wise adults recognize they need to remain the limit setters and not try to join the club or gain entry by relinquishing the role of grown-up in charge. Respect is more valuable and harder to come by than camaraderie. The more the young adult is in emotional turmoil, the more he or she needs clear limits and high expectations. Although students may not admit it—at least at the time—the class and the individuals in it feel safer if they know the rules and what to expect.

With respect comes the ability to influence the social dynamics and loyalties among your students. Although they can be cruel to someone who is different, they can be even tougher defending someone who might otherwise be left out of a circle. When you insist on inclusion and provide support to allow a student with special needs to achieve to fullest potential with dignity, your behavior sets a benchmark for students. Your approach can turn egocentric peer pressure into energetic peer support. It may be tough work, but when you succeed, you know why you choose to teach at middle school.

Encourage your students to appreciate that science is a social endeavor. Give students opportunities to assess their own abilities and request the specific assistance they need. Convey confidence that every student can achieve all standards, albeit in different ways and by differing means. Encourage students to understand they are responsible, not only for their own safety, but for the safety of all others in their group and in their classroom. They'll be better scientists for it.

THE SAVVY SCIENCE TEACHER

Two of Ms. A's life science sections are co-taught; she partners with Mr. C, a special education teacher with expertise in learning disabilities. The teachers share a planning period and regularly rotate the responsibilities of lead teacher. One day each week, Mr. C helps students with informational reading. He prepares different study sheets for various ability groups in the class: open-ended exploration, structured reading (with blanks), and specially designed two-choice worksheets for students with limited reading disability. This special help Mr. C offers is subtle and protective of middle school egos. On test days, Mr. C provides oral help in a separate room, but all students participate equally in every other activity. When labs are planned, the students rotate through cooperative groups. If one of Mr. C's identified students draws the role of recorder, he's there to assist, even though personal word processors with spell checkers make success the common denominator.

Connections

▶ American Chemical Society. 2001. *Chemical Safety for Teachers and Their Supervisors.* Washington, DC: American Chemical Society.
▶ *www.safeschoolsamerica. com/StandardsList.htm*
▶ *www.ibiblio.org/nppa/ sherer/sherer12.html*
▶ Science Education for Students with Disabilities. *www.as.wvu.edu/~scidis/ organizations/index.html*

Where Science Happens

Equipping Your Lab for Safety

By midsummer, Ms. M was eager to check on progress at Clement Street Middle School, due to open in three weeks. She arrived just as contractors were installing the Clement Street Middle School sign over the old Memorial High School sign. Making her way down newly painted hallways, she noticed that fire doors with automatic emergency releases had replaced the old swinging doors. In her assigned room, she was pleased to see her file cabinet had been delivered but was a little taken aback by the rest of the furnishings. The old lab stations had been replaced by rows of tablet-arm chairs. Perimeter sinks had been repaired, but, instead of the six new four-student worktables she had requested, she found tables from the elementary school that were too low to be pulled up to the perimeter workstations. Good thing she had come early to check, she thought.

Making Room for Science

Unless your middle school facility was built fewer than 20 years ago, chances are it was originally designed and built for another purpose. Often, the middle school building had been the solution to an enrollment or facility problem, not an educational concept. Older middle school buildings are frequently renovated or converted elementary, primary, junior high, and high school buildings. But for inquiry-based middle school science, the configuration and condition of science facilities are important components of a safe and successful program.

Government studies have indicated that more than 40 percent of school buildings are in such poor condition they are unsafe for the occupants. Even new facilities can be too crowded or architecturally unsuited for science exploration. It's important to know the recommended facilities standards for middle school science, whether or not those ideal conditions can be achieved right away. You can set goals and modify your program as you work toward the recommended standards.

Although most elementary school science can and should be carried on in well-outfitted self-contained classrooms, middle school science is a rigorous investigation-based program that involves activities that require specialized facilities. There should be specifically designated rooms for science classes, including, for instance, two exits, multiple sink facilities, a safety eyewash and safety shower, lockable storage for chemicals and specialized equipment, flat chemical-resistant surfaces, in-room fire protection, enhanced electrical service, equipment to enlarge and project organisms or reactions, data display areas, and places for projects that need to be kept intact over an extended period for experimentation and observation. Furthermore, the middle school science room is likely to contain equipment, supplies, and organisms that would make it an unwise site for nonscience classes.

Ideally, science teachers should have their own rooms that can be set up to support laboratory activities as well as discussion and large-group instruction. Middle school labs need not last an entire period, but some investigational work should occur almost every day—frequently on an impromptu basis as class discussions give rise to opportunities for rechecking observations or investigating new theories. Scheduling sessions in a shared lab while spending most of the time in a room not outfitted for laboratory work is awkward and results in many missed opportunities. It is also unsafe; the teacher ends up setting up labs and then leaving the room empty or in use by others. If a science class must be scheduled in a nonscience space, then consider using portable lab stations with locked storage space.

Space and Class Size—Keys to Safety

Ensuring sufficient space in the classroom/laboratory is a critical component of maintaining a safe science program. Another is limiting the number of students in the science class. Middle schoolers are experiencing tremendous physical growth and body changes. Responding to their age and raging hormones, middle school students are characteristically more daring and less inhibited than either elementary students or high school students. Although sufficient space and smaller classes do not guarantee safety, the data are clear: When the space per student goes down or class size goes up, the accident rate goes up. Minimum space requirements are listed in the box, "Take Out Your Tape Measure." Ideally, science classes should have no more than 24 students. When space requirements cannot be met, limit enrollment even further. If you cannot expand space or limit enrollment close to the recommended standards, then you must document the specific labs and program elements that you cannot do safely, notify the appropriate administrators, and, most important, *perform only those activities that are safest for the conditions you have*.

Take a few minutes to look around. Can you supervise every area where students can be working? If not, consider rearranging your furniture and adding strategically placed parabolic mirrors. Can students get to the sink or eyewash within 10 seconds? If not, give some of the furniture to another school site. Even the most spacious classrooms can be cluttered by excess furniture. Teachers can be pack rats, saving stuff just in case, with collections becoming safety hazards and reducing working space. Keep no more than one steel filing cabinet of old papers and plans. Scan your favorite exercises onto a CD-ROM and get rid of the paper. Do not block escape routes or routes to safety showers and eyewash stations.

Warning

You must document safety problems and see to it this information is communicated to the appropriate authorities, but this does not relieve you of responsibility. If you know an activity is unsafe and still perform it with your students, you can be held liable for purposefully and knowingly placing students in danger. Documenting a safety problem in writing is strong evidence you know an activity is dangerous. You do not want to hear an attorney say, "So you continued to do a dangerous lab even though you knew the facility was not equipped to do it safely?" See Chapter 11 for more information concerning liability.

Come in early one morning and conduct imaginary emergency drills: In case of fire, is there enough room to stop, drop, and roll? Could everyone get out quickly? Remember that a fire door could close automatically, slowing down a disabled student. In case of an accidental spill, can students back out of the way of the splash or clear the area? If a splash should occur at any of the work areas, is there a quick clear path to a sink, safety shower, or eyewash?

All on the Same Team

As frustrating as it may be, schools probably will always have more problems and limitations than resources to solve them. Physical facilities are likely to be the most expensive and daunting problem of all with extensive renovation and new construction years away.

But remember there are many partners in the educational enterprise. You and your teaching colleagues are part of the team; so are the administrators, parents, and school board members. These other team members may be even more frustrated than you when new construction or renovation cannot happen even when badly needed. So you need to work as a partner in the educational enterprise by clearly documenting and communicating your needs and the restrictions that must be put in place if physical conditions cannot be changed. Keep in mind that, as the content and discipline specialist, you know the concepts and skills that are important, and you are the person most likely to have the information and preparation to suggest alternatives for ameliorating the situation.

Most schools begin to schedule and plan purchases for the following school year before the end of the current school year—some as early as December or January. Find out when planning starts, and schedule a planning meeting with the administrator-in-charge. Lobby hard to keep science class sizes at no more than 24 students, and make it clear that adding extra desks won't solve a crowding problem. Make your presentation positive, showing what key concepts can be taught more effectively and what new experiences can be introduced with smaller class sizes and suitable facilities. But be very clear about what cannot be done if the proper conditions are not available. Identify curricular activities that are unsafe in a crowded situation. Be prepared with alternative suggestions, and work with your beleaguered administrators. Consider the possibility that the administration is saying "no" because they can't think of any way to solve your problem. If you are flexible and creative and take the lead in suggesting minor facility alterations, portable equipment, alternative activities, and scheduling strategies that can support the strongest investigative program possible with the resources available, you can solve many of your problems.

Packing Relief

Packing up and moving your room may be the opportunity of a lifetime. Be ruthless. Do not move anything you can do without. Do not seal any cartons containing items you have failed to subject to hard scrutiny. Less is better, and, if you don't look it over now, you probably never will.

When your school is finally scheduled for new construction or major renovation, participating in the design and planning of the facility is well worth your time. As expert as the design specialists may be, you want to be sure your architects do not design your science facilities for the program they remember having when they were in junior high school. For new construction suggestions, refer to *NSTA Guide to School Science Facilities* (Biehle, Motz, and West 1999), and consider making a copy available to the administrators and architects who will take the lead in the project.

Building for the Future

If you have contractors on site for renovations, you also have special challenges for your program and for the safety of your students. It is important to communicate your program needs to the on-site supervisors.

Your school's renovation project should have an on-site supervisor who is familiar with the site and can act on behalf of everyone who must continue to work in the building. Make sure the responsible contact person is aware of special considerations for maintaining safety for your science program.

Be conscious of ventilation patterns that might be disrupted. If your room will be temporarily less well ventilated, or if you will have less natural light, modify your program accordingly.

Make sure the construction contact person is aware of any potentially hazardous materials or equipment present in your classroom—especially those things that could be harmful to construction workers if there were a spill or other emergency.

You will probably need to make adjustments to your program because of conditions caused by a construction project going on simultaneously. Most of these adjustments should have been planned well ahead of time, but some may be needed because of unforeseen conditions.

Look over the year's plans with an eye towards simplifying and refocusing some of the activities. You are likely to find you will not be able to accomplish as much in your science program. You and your students may be more distracted, exhausted, or both as the construction project extends beyond a few weeks or a couple of months. On days when excessive noise or other disruptions are predicted, consider taking your classes outdoors for fieldwork or off site on a field trip. Above all, be flexible and maintain a sense of humor.

Consider using the construction project as an opportunity to reinforce safety concepts. Give students a tour around the limits of the work and explain where they may not go. Ask them to report any stray tools, nails, or other products.

Safety During Construction

In rooms to be used during construction, the following safety issues must be addressed:

- Creating effective sound and dust barriers
- Maintaining required fresh air flow
- Maintaining unobstructed emergency escape routes
- Maintaining ground fault interrupter protection and correct carrying load of electrical service
- Maintaining integrity of alarm and communications systems
- Ensuring accessibility and operability of safety equipment—fire extinguishers, emergency showers and eyewashes, ventilation of chemical storage cabinets
- Planning for the protection of equipment in place and when moved
- Appropriately handling potentially hazardous materials and supplies

3

You may be able to invite the on-site supervisor, project architect, or a master builder to come and describe their jobs and the safety precautions that must be taken at the site. (See Chapter 11, p. 150, "Guests and Others.")

NO NEWS CAN BE BETTER

Bay Middle School thought its long construction project was at an end until one Monday morning when a strange odor wafted down the halls. No one could identify the smell, but everyone knew it was unpleasant. Rumors spread like wildfire: It was toxic. It was corrosive.

Reacting to the rumors, teachers and children began to cover their faces, and soon several sensitive students were gasping. A visiting parent called a local news channel; another called 911. Soon reporters, police, and ambulances were hovering, and the whole school had to be evacuated. A dozen students were treated for possible respiratory distress.

Meanwhile, the principal was investigating. The previous Saturday, contractors had applied a coat of sealer on the concrete under an overhead fan. What was the chemical? No one knew. No material safety data sheet (MSDS) was available. Hours later the errant workers were tracked down, the chemical identified, and its very low toxicity documented. It was a harmless—but odorous—varnish, and only a very small quantity had been applied. Because the weekend had been rainy, it hadn't dried, and its location under a fan had made the odor spread. A single MSDS on the principal's desk would have prevented a countywide emergency and a major public relations fiasco.

Behind the Labels

You are responsible for *every* material you bring into or accept in your classroom. Make sure you know what it is, what it can do, and how it should be stored. You are also responsible for ensuring that others in the building, such as the custodian and principal, know this information ahead of time before an emergency occurs. The federal government requires that all manufacturers supply material safety data sheets (MSDS) for every substance they produce. These documents are in a standard format and should be obtained for every material you order—including markers, cleaning supplies, glues, and paints. Don't allow anything to be stored before you have them. Keep copies of the MSDSs in the office and in your classroom. Your central office and local fire department should also maintain a list of all potentially hazardous materials so they can properly respond to emergencies. For more information on MSDSs, see Chapter 4, p. 41. Do not ask students to bring in chemicals and other materials from home, because it is unlikely they could bring an MSDS for them and they may not be transported safely. Do not accept chemicals from high school or college colleagues, parents, businesses, or any other generous donors. You cannot be sure of their age, purity, or other characteristics.

3

BEWARE THE GEEK BEARING GIFTS

To save yourself from liability, responsibility, and a lot of expensive and unrewarding work, never accept gifts or donations of chemicals from well-meaning parents, upper-grade teachers, business and industry, or anyone else. You will not have the appropriate MSDS documents, and you cannot be certain of the age, purity, and prior storage conditions of chemicals that are not ordered and received directly from a reliable science supply house. Some donors even make "gifts" only to rid themselves of the responsibility of hazardous waste disposal. Some materials may not be subject to regulations when you first accept them, but may be declared hazardous after you have accepted them. The responsibility and cost for hazardous waste disposal becomes yours. (See Chapter 4, p. 45, for more information.)

Secure all your chemical stocks, discuss potential hazards, and teach students to respect chemicals. Teachers have been held liable for serious accidents when students stole chemicals from unlocked cabinets and used them to make explosions at home. (See Chapter 4, p. 49, for true stories.) Do not allow students to handle concentrated chemicals, and limit cleaning supplies to dish soap and vinegar solutions.

SCI*LINKS.
THE WORLD'S A CLICK AWAY
Topic: chemical safety
Go to: *www.scilinks.org*
Code: SML29

Let the Sunshine In

Remember when renovators were covering up school windows to save heat? Now researchers tell us there is strong evidence student achievement is higher in natural light. We also know that some fluorescent lights exacerbate hyperactivity and headaches and make computer screens more difficult to read.

Lighting is also a factor in maintaining safety. Make sure your storage areas, deep cabinets, and corners are well lit. Investigate whether your escape routes would be visible if the power fails. Some schools have emergency backup lighting for this purpose. Keep flashlights handy and check batteries periodically.

Fire Protection

To meet building codes, schools are required to have features for fire prevention and fire protection. New buildings have sprinkler systems; most have double exits and main floor escape routes. But even the best design can be defeated by thoughtless use. Recognizing the safety features of your physical facilities and ensuring that access to them is not hampered are important.

SCI*LINKS.*
THE WORLD'S A CLICK AWAY

Topic: fire extinguishers
Go to: *www.scilinks.org*
Code: SML30

Your classroom was probably designed to have two emergency exits. One may be a large window without a screen. Have you screened that window? Have you blocked a fire exit with furniture? Have you scheduled science activities with fire or chemical hazards in a location with fewer than two exits? The wall coverings and ceilings of your classroom are fire resistant. Have you covered them with paper or hung other combustible materials from the walls or ceilings? Make sure that hanging projects and displays conform to district policy and fire codes.

HEAT WITHOUT FIRE

Open flames are not recommended for middle school. A flameless heating system such as laboratory-rated hot plates or warm water baths can substitute. If you need a flame, consider using a candle that is wider than it is tall—tea lights are a possibility. Alcohol burners should never be used. They pose multiple unnecessary hazards—unnoticed cracks can cause a burner to explode, improper filling can result in flash backs and explosions, and alcohol supply cans are a major hazard both in use and in storage.

You need an ABC fire extinguisher for your science classroom. It should have a nylon or wire seal and a tag indicating the most recent inspection date. Notify your building administrator if the tag is missing or the inspection is not up to date. Show every student where the fire extinguisher is located, and make sure everyone knows how to use it. Ensure that the smoke detector and fire alarm are not obscured or blocked from access. Teach your students to recognize the visual and audio fire alarm signals and to respond to them immediately. In a science class, this means stopping work right away and turning off equipment in the immediate work area. Post the fire escape route, and regularly practice using it. Make sure students know the difference between the procedures following a fire alarm and the procedures for windstorms, earthquakes, or other emergencies.

Before any lab exercise that involves flame or heat, teach students how to respond if their hair or clothing catches fire—they must not run or do anything that will fan the flames—and have them practice "stop, drop, and roll." If you have a fire blanket or safety shower, teach their proper use and review the use of safety equipment before every instance where this equipment might be needed.

See if your local firefighters would make a courtesy inspection to advise you and your class on making your facilities and lab practices safer. If they are willing, review your expectations with the visiting personnel ahead of the visit. See Chapter 11, p. 151 ,"Classroom Guests."

A Partnership with Your Student Scientists

Scientists use specialized equipment to do their investigations. Your students will respect their science experiences more if they are partners in the inventory, storage, and safekeeping of that equipment in your classroom. Middle school students are especially suited for these new responsibilities.

Experts recommend a separate, lockable preparation space for science teachers. It should be well ventilated, preferably with direct outdoor air exchange. Whether or not this is possible, invest in vented, locked cabinets for all of your chemicals. Corrosives, flammables, toxic (poisonous) chemicals, and reactive chemicals should have separate storage. Cabinets for volatile chemicals should be vented. Shelves should have lips to prevent spills. Corners should be rounded to reduce injuries. Glass doors are not recommended for cabinets, both because of the potential for breaking and because the contents may look too tempting.

Store chemicals by category, not alphabetically. (See Chapter 4, p. 39, for more information.) Date your acquisitions, and dispose of old stock correctly. Keep only what you need, and don't accept hand-me-downs or donations from the high school, parents, industry, or anywhere else.

Prepare chemicals for labs before the students arrive. Remove only the quantity of the chemicals you will be using, and keep the stock bottles locked up during class. A suggested middle school chemical inventory is listed in Chapter 6, p. 84.

Power Up

When teachers are asked to identify unmet needs in their classrooms, space is often their first concern, but electric service ranks a close second. As we add more electronic devices to our programs, there never seem to be enough electrical receptacles in the right places.

Your room should have at least four separate circuits, each protected by ground fault interrupters (GFI) that automatically cut off power to prevent shock. If you are tripping circuit breakers, you don't have enough circuits to handle your current needs. This happens most often when you are drawing power for heating or cooling devices, such as hot plates and air conditioners. Remember, you can't just add receptacles—you must add circuits to solve the power problem. Do not use the "socket multipliers" that are sold in hardware stores, because they will only increase the load on existing circuits.

Extension cords pose both fire and tripping hazards. Never allow loose cords to cross aisles and pathways or use extension cords for permanent installations. If floor receptacles project above the floor, make sure furniture above them prevents anyone from tripping over them. Flat floor receptacles must seal completely so spills can't enter. Spring-loaded rollers that allow cords to be pulled from the ceiling are sometimes good options. Consult an architect or your school facilities supervisor for help getting the power you need—don't try to fix the situation yourself.

Furniture and Fixtures

A well-designed middle school science classroom should allow a smooth flow from seat work to lab work and back again. Six sink stations installed around the perimeter of the room work well for 24 students. If you have the opportunity to select your furnishings, consider flexibility and safety together—they are compatible goals. Sturdy two-student flat surface worktables are preferable to permanently installed casework. At the middle school level, specify science-style tables with chemical-resistant tops and non-adjustable legs, making the height of the tables match the height of countertops where sinks are installed. Vary the height of stools rather than the height of tables. The ideal tables are light enough to be pulled up to perimeter workstations or rearranged in the middle of the room for different activities, but solid enough to remain steady and immovable during lab work. Use standing-height tables and perimeter counters for chemistry, Earth science, and physical science work, although seated height may be more compatible with life science observation. If you are ordering tall—standing height—tables, select a style with sturdy legs and reinforcing stretcher bars near the base to stabilize the legs.

Avoid the use of stools during laboratory work. Having students stand during hands-on activities is much safer in case of a spill. If you have stools, remove the backs to make it more difficult for students to tip back and balance on two legs. Some classrooms have lab stations without chairs on the perimeter. This may require a larger total classroom perimeter, but keeps students from being distracted by lab equipment during direct instruction and other seat work time.

Make sure you have enough space, adequate exits and ventilation, and hot and cold running water. Request natural lighting and extra parabolic (nonreflective) lights for close work. Include an eyewash and shower, and a sink with a wet—tiled—area for cleanup.

Special equipment and other aids needed to ensure a safe environment for special needs students should be identified in individual education plans (IEPs). These plans should be carefully reviewed in planning for the physical space as well as for instructional strategies.

Signs and Symbols

Labeling in your classroom can make it both educational and safe. First, make sure your room number is clearly identified and your students know what it is in case of emergency. Post important emergency phone numbers and extensions right beside the fire, storm, and earthquake procedures. Practice identifying the pictograms you plan to use. Some typical symbols:

Make signage an integral part of your room organization plan. Label where things go and where they don't go. Use lots of pictures and symbols as well as worded labels and instructions. Use bilingual signage if it is needed in your school. Keep charts for maintenance and organism-care responsibilities. Let your students know where your fire protection equipment is and when it is maintained. Keep eye protection on display with signs describing its use and cleaning. Mark the shower, eyewash, and fire extinguisher areas, and keep them clear.

Clear markings contribute to clear thinking. They also convey the idea that safety is a shared responsibility for all science investigators.

| Poison | Combustible | Biohazard |
| Explosive | High Voltage | Corrosive |

Bricks and Mortar

Facilities are the least flexible part of a school program. Although there may be long-term remodeling goals for most buildings, many teachers find their current situation very limited. What do you do if you know your classroom doesn't meet safety and facility standards and there is no immediate relief in sight?

First, clean up and clean out. Make space by removing everything you don't need from the room. You may need to box up materials by month or season. Then take a hard look at your furnishings. Can you invest in more flexible pieces or trade with another teacher? Can you rearrange to create more space?

Prioritize your maintenance requests and *document them*. Don't fall victim to the "they won't do it anyway" attitude. Repeat your requests at regular intervals, and explain to your administrator what choices you are forced to make until you can get repairs made.

National Science Teachers Associatio

Downsize your lab experiences and your storage needs. Then remember that science is *everywhere*. Take your students outside to study not just biology but physics. Use grocery store materials to study chemistry. See Chapter 9, p. 109, for more suggestions. Be creative while you are being safe. Document what you cannot do safely for your administrator.

THE SAVVY SCIENCE TEACHER

Seventh grade teacher Mr. D found he would be sharing storage space with the eighth grade physical science teacher. Before he moved in, he requested separate, lockable chemical cabinets. His needs were different and his concentrations much lower than those in the eighth grade program. He divided the glassware cabinet too. He explained he was very willing to share, but it would take extra effort to make absolutely sure there wasn't any cross-contamination.

Mr. D's middle school classroom was smaller and had more desks than his elementary room. He quickly calculated his largest class and moved the extra desks out in the hall. A quick note to the principal justified the move—space to maneuver, space for safety.

Mr. D's inventory moved with him and so did his collection of MSDSs. His models and displays came too. His program thrives wherever he goes because it is developmentally appropriate. Preplanning and good communication ensure it retains its safe character.

Connections

- Biehle, J., L. Motz, and S. West. 1999. *NSTA Guide to School Science Facilities.* Arlington, VA: NSTA Press.
- Lowery, L., ed. 2000. Appendix C in *NSTA Pathways to the Science Standards—Elementary School Edition.* Arlington, VA: NSTA Press.

Finders Keepers
Essentials of Safer Storage

Like most delayed building projects, Midvale High School was completed only a month before opening day. This meant the middle school staff had less than two weeks to move into the large old building the high school staff was abandoning. When they arrived, some teachers thought they had been given a bonus. The high school staff had left many "treasures" behind in their rush to move. In the science department alone, there were rock samples, aquaria, and all sorts of chemicals. A quick look in the storage room revealed a half-used gallon container of concentrated nitric acid, an old mercury barometer, and a shelf full of chemicals that had been left by the high school chemistry department. On the floor was a bucket filled with preserved frogs.

Finders keepers? The middle school science department faced a dilemma: Were their newly discovered supplies valuable? More important, were they safe? And, if not, who would take care of disposal?

The Stuff of Science

I t takes a lot of "stuff" to conduct a middle school science program. Students who are progressing from concrete to formal logic need an environment full of materials to handle, observe, and manipulate. They will explore these things with all the energy characteristic of their age in an environment with newly expanded freedoms.

Middle school science teachers look enviously at their peers in the English department who neatly carry everything they need for class in a single tote bag. The science teacher, on the other hand, is always loaded down with supplies, stopping for last-minute items at the local convenience store, and hoarding all sorts of things that might come in handy some day. But saving things also requires a lot of storage. It's the smart middle school science teacher who knows how to balance what must be saved with what can be stored.

4

37

Recycled Quarters

Middle schools are often the ignored middle child in growing districts. Recycled older buildings are frequently renamed "middle school" as the population expands. These facilities may not be suitably designed for new middle school programs and active preadolescent students. If this is your situation, you must be especially conscious of storage issues and the potential hazards if your supplies are not safely and securely stored. While advocating for the space you need, you must strike a balance between those truly useful items that can be stored neatly and safely and unneeded items—the just-in-case collection.

Many times, regular classrooms are turned into science labs. These rooms are often smaller than needed for an active science program. With the addition of cabinets, there is even less usable space. (Refer to "Take Out Your Tape Measure," p. 24, in Chapter 3 for minimum space requirements.) If this is your situation, recommend the purchase of smaller, multipurpose furniture or trade. For computers, consider laptops rather than desktop systems. Reduce the numbers and sizes of cages, planters, and models. Opt for small animals and small terraria. If you have a television or projection screen, mount it on the wall or ceiling rather than adding more loose furniture. Find a safe place somewhere else in the school to store the models, books, and other pieces of equipment needed only occasionally.

Scope Creep

Middle schools have a condition not found at levels above or below it—scope creep. This disease has two sets of symptoms. First, there's the district that constantly changes its definition of what a middle school is: One year the ninth grade is in, the next year it is out. You know you've fallen victim to scope creep when you hear yourself say: "We'd better save that silver nitrate, because we may need it again if they put ninth grade back." In its alternate form, scope creep takes a psychological turn: "This lab was so much fun when I did it in high school or college, my middle school students will love it." This form may be based on the false assumption that students are capable of understanding what they enjoy watching.

Both forms of scope creep have similar side effects: Middle school teachers tend to store materials that aren't necessary for a sound program, overestimating the conceptual levels of their students and underestimating the potential for accidents. It is too easy to forget what is developmentally appropriate. Luckily, both forms of the condition have the same cure: a rigorous survey and cleanout that results in the elimination and proper disposal of everything that doesn't belong.

Safety by Design

If you are fortunate enough to be able to influence the design of a new building or a classroom renovation, be sure consideration is given to storage. Experts recommend three square meters or more of storage and preparation space for each student in the class. Ideally, there should be a well-ventilated preparation room or area for teachers only, separate from the storage room. Stock bottles should be kept in storage and preparation areas. Only well-labeled smaller quantities of chemicals—just enough for the proposed activity—should be brought into student work areas.

In-class storage should be provided for glassware, models, and other nonconsumable equipment. Ideally, storage should be distributed throughout the room, occupying space on at least three of the four walls. Because middle school students can help with the distribution and storage of equipment, provide labels and organizational diagrams.

Include flat storage drawers to store posters and charts, space for tall items such as meter sticks, and larger spaces for models and bulky equipment. Avoid glass doors on cabinets. They are breakable and tempting and almost always make cabinets look messy. Prevent spills by having lips on the edges of cabinets. Choose cabinets and equipment that have rounded rather than sharp corners and edges. You might want to use tote drawers or dish tubs to store and distribute all items needed for a particular activity or for each student work team. Include a laminated card with a list of the supplies and safety precautions. This type of setup can be very convenient for lab setup and cleanup and for visual learners and absentees.

Most state and local building codes require that nonmovable cabinets be anchored to the wall so they cannot possibly cause injury in a tipping accident. Even if there is no such code in your district, check all your cabinet and storage units for proper stability and insist on anchoring the units. Movable carts may also be prone to tipping, especially tall ones such as those used for large televisions or video displays. Be sure to lock and anchor movable equipment carefully and check for stability before attempting to move it.

Lock Them Up

Cabinets used for storing chemicals must have secure locks, and students should never have the keys, even for a short time. If chemicals must be stored in active student space, the cabinet should never be left unlocked when students are present. Make chemical security a habit. Take out small amounts of needed chemicals before

Storing Chemicals

▶ Chemical supplies must be in securely locked cabinets, preferably in securely locked rooms separate from student work areas.

▶ Shelves for chemical storage should have lips or fences to prevent bottles from falling off, especially important in earthquake zones. Dowels installed about 2 cm above the ledge can serve this purpose.

▶ Chemicals should be stored by compatibility and not alphabetically. Flammables and corrosive chemicals require their own cabinets.

▶ Never store combustible materials such as paper supplies and rags with chemicals.

▶ Do not keep corrosives (e.g., acids and bases) that are stronger than you need. These items belong in locked corrosion-resistant cabinets.

▶ If a chemical storage cabinet must be located in a student space, make sure it is locked and anchored to the wall so it cannot be toppled or accessed by an unauthorized person.
(cont. next page)

class, put the stock bottles away, and lock them up. Labeled medicine dose cups or party candy cups make great containers for dispensing small quantities of chemicals.

There are special cabinets for corrosive chemicals such as acids and bases. They are made of special materials resistant to chemical corrosion. Storage for volatile chemicals should be ventilated and requires special installation. If your program requires acids, bases, or other potentially corrosive chemicals, it is better to purchase small prediluted quantities and consider alternatives to lab activities that require strong chemicals. (See Chapter 6, p. 76, for some safer alternatives.) Review all of your lab activities to see if they can be done as microchemistry units. A microchemistry approach uses small amounts of chemicals, droppers, and clear plastic plates with test wells that reveal changes clearly and wash up quickly.

Flammable liquids require fireproof storage space. If you don't have a well-ventilated storage area, keep flammable chemicals such as rubbing alcohol in a flameproof section of custodial storage. Never store paper or rags in the same space. If you are unsure about the properties of a chemical, check the side of the bottle where symbols should be present to indicate the hazards of the chemical. (See hazards symbols in Chapter 3, p. 34.) Store toxic chemicals separately as well.

And just because you now know how to store corrosives, reactives, flammables, and toxins does not mean they should be there. Store the minimum.

Age Discrimination

Chemicals are not like fine wines. They do not grow better as they age. Many are reactive, unstable, or decompose to become very dangerous. Consider just a few examples:

▶ Ethers, highly volatile and flammable to begin with, can react with oxygen in air to form peroxides so unstable that just turning the cap can cause an explosion.

▶ Picric acid was once used to preserve specimens. It becomes an unstable explosive when dried out, however, and should not be used below the college level. If you should find picric acid or suspect something could be picric acid, do not touch or move it, and evacuate the area immediately. Just jarring it can cause it to explode. Call immediately for professionally trained help with removal and disposal.

▶ Many powdered reagents become so hard they cannot be removed from their stock bottles. Attempting to break up a chunk can cause some chemicals to explode.

Date every purchase. Buy only what you need for one year, even if it's cheaper to buy in quantity. Consider the costs and hazards of disposal before you purchase, and get rid of all old chemicals properly at the end of the year. Your curriculum might change, program needs might be different, or you might have another assignment. Share this important principle with the administration; they need to budget for new consumables each year.

Storing Chemicals (cont.)

▶ Keep a notebook of material safety data sheets (MSDSs) with the purchase date, storage conditions, and disposal instructions for each chemical. Provide a copy of the chemical inventory for your office and another for your local fire department.
▶ Write the telephone number of the nearest Poison Control Center in front of your lesson plan book and telephone book, and post it near your classroom intercom or telephone.

4

Material Safety Data Sheets

A material safety data sheet (MSDS) is a standard document available for every chemical manufactured or sold in the United States. It contains specific information in a specific format so that teacher, chemist, doctor, and emergency medical technician can find what they need immediately. Many teachers don't realize that MSDSs are available for such common chemicals as glue, paste, soap, and markers as well as exotic chemicals.

Federal and many state laws require that MSDSs be available all the time for every chemical you use or store in your classroom. Administrative and noninstructional staff, teacher and students, and emergency personnel who might enter the building must have easy access to them. That normally means there should be at least two complete sets of documents, one in the classroom and one in the office. Your

SCI LINKS.
THE WORLD'S A CLICK AWAY

Topic: chemical safety
Go to: *www.scilinks.org*
Code: SML29

local fire department should also be provided with an inventory and a map showing the specific location of the MSDSs.

You may be surprised to learn that "every chemical" includes common, everyday items such as markers, dish and hand soaps, and even food materials such as baking soda. When chemicals are ordered through normal school supply vendors, your requisition should specify that the vendor "Provide MSDS with order." Your school office personnel should be told to look for and file the MSDS, because they may be the ones to accept packages. They must insist that the MSDSs come in each shipment—or refuse to accept it. When a supply such as glue is available for teachers to take from the office, there should be multiple copies of the MSDS alongside to take with the material. If you take supplies from the office, you need to take the MSDS along. If other groups or teachers use your classroom, you need to let other users know the location of the MSDSs.

If you need to bring chemicals from home or purchase them at a convenience store because they are less expensive, you must get the MSDS yourself. You can sometimes find a telephone number on the bottle. A good source of MSDS information for common household products is the Vermont SIRI site. (See Connections at the end of this chapter.)

MATERIAL SAFETY DATA SHEET—BLEACH LAUNDRY ORGANIC CHLORINE

(Abbreviated version)

General Information

Item Name: BLEACH LAUNDRY ORGANIC CHLORINE
Company's Name and Address: _____
Company's Emerg Ph #: _____

Ingredients/Identity Information

Proprietary: NO Signs/Symptoms Of Overexp: INHALATION: IRRITATION TO NOSE, THROAT, MOUTH SEVERE IRRITATION AND/OR BURNS. EYES: SEVERE IRRITATION AND/OR BURNS CAN OCCUR.
Emergency/First Aid Proc: EYES: FLUSH W/LG AMTS WATER—15 MIN, OCCASIONALLY LIFT UPPER/LOWER LIDS. CALL DOCTOR. SKIN: FLUSH—15 MIN. CALL DOCTOR. REMOVE CONTAM CLOTHING AND WASH BEFORE REUSE. INGEST: DON'T INDUCE VOMIT. DRINK LG AMTS WATER. DON'T GIVE ANYTHING BY MOUTH IF PERSON IS UNCONSCIOUS OR HAVING CONVULSIONS. INHALE: REMOVE TO FRESH AIR. IF BREATH HARD, GIVE OXY. KEEP WARM/REST. IF BREATH STOPS, GIVE CPR. CALL DOCTOR.

Precautions for Safe Handling and Use

Steps If Matl Released/Spill: IF SPILL IS DRY, CLEAN UP W/CLEAN, DRY DEDICATED EQUIP & PLACE IN CLEAN, DRY CNTNR. SPILL RESIDUES: DISPOSE OF (cont.)

MATERIAL SAFETY DATA SHEET—BLEACH LAUNDRY ORGANIC CHLORINE
(Abbreviated version, cont.)

AS NOTED BELOW. NEUTRALIZE MAT'L FOR DISPOSAL. CALL 1-800-654-6911
Waste Disposal Method: PRODUCT DOES NOT MEET CRITERIA OF HAZARDOUS
WASTE. AS A NONHAZARDOUS SOLID WASTE, DISPOSE OF PER LOCAL, STATE, &
FEDERAL REGULATIONS BY TREATMENT IN A WASTEWATER TREATMENT CENTER.

TAKE CARE TO PREVENT CONTAMINATION FROM THE USE OF THIS PRODUCT.
COOL, DRY, WELL-VENT AREA. DO NOT STORE ABOVE 140 F OR IN PAPER/
CARDBOARD. KEEP CLOSED & FROM MOISTURE.
Other Precautions: ADDITIONAL RESPIRATORY PROTECTION NECESSARY WHEN
SMALL, DAMP SPILLS INVOLVING PRODUCT OCCUR, WHICH RELEASES
CHLORINE GAS. FULL FACE CARTRIDGE-TYPE NIOSH APPROVED RESPIRATORY
W/CHLORINE CARTRIDGE RECOMMENDED. USE SELF-CNTND BREATHING
APPAR.Ingredient: SODIUM CHLORIDE
Ingredient Sequence Number: 01
Percent: 45-50

Proprietary: NO
Ingredient: SODIUM TRIPOLYPHOSPHATE
Ingredient Sequence Number: 02
Percent: 25-30

Proprietary: NO
Ingredient: SODIUM DICHLORO-S-TRIAZINETRIONE
Ingredient Sequence Number: 03
Percent: 24-28

Fire and Explosion Hazard Data

Extinguishing Media: USE MEDIA TO CONTROL A SURROUNDING FIRE. DO NOT
USE DRY CHEMICAL EXTINGUISHERS CONTAINING AMMONIUM COMPOUNDS.
Special Fire Fighting Proc: USE WATER TO COOL CONTAINERS EXPOSED TO FIRE.
SMALL FIRES—USE WATER SPRAY OR FOG. LARGE FIRES—USE HEAVY DELUGE OR
FOG STREAMS.
Unusual Fire And Expl Hazrds: NONE. REQUIRED BEFORE EXTINGUISHMENT CAN
BE ACCOMPLISHED. THE USE OF SELF-CONTAINED BREATHING APPARATUS IS
REQUIRED IN A FIRE WHERE THIS PRODUCT IS INVOLVED.

Reactivity Data

Stability: YES
Cond To Avoid (Stability): ELEVATED TEMPERATURES (ABOVE 140 F)
Materials To Avoid: OTHER OXIDIZERS, NITROGEN CONTAINING COMPOUNDS,
DRY FIRE EXTINGUISHERS CONTAINING MONO-AMMONIUM PHOSPHATE.
Hazardous Decomp Products: NITROGEN TRICHLORIDE, CHLORINE, CARBON
MONOXIDE.
(cont.)

4

The Itinerant Teacher

In overcrowded middle schools, teachers may be assigned to different classrooms for different periods—science on a cart. This practice greatly increases the chance for accidents. A rotating teacher is never sure of what may have been left out from the class before or what may linger on a desk or counter. Teachers do not have access to set up the room and the supplies properly. When one teacher leaves and the other has not yet arrived, the classroom/lab is often unsupervised. Even worse, the newest, least-experienced teacher is frequently the one required to rotate through the classrooms of veteran teachers when the veteran teachers have their prep periods.

The ideal situation is to have each science teacher assigned to one science classroom and to have schedules in which similar classes, or preps, are grouped sequentially. Then chemicals are stored at point of use. When this isn't possible, teachers and administrators should work together, take a hard look at the program, and make modifications that are necessary to ensure safety. If a teacher *must* rotate, it should be the most experienced teacher that does so. Whatever the conditions and the schedules, safe and secure storage must be provided for science supplies and equipment—even if some of this storage is in the form of lockable portable units. There is potential for liability if chemicals and specialized equipment are not properly stored and secured.

If you must change rooms during the day, ask for the strong, lockable, movable units that can travel with you. Be certain they have lockable wheels that keep them solidly in place. Bring only the minimum with you. Stock bottles should still be kept in a locked permanent storage area rather than in movable carts.

If you are an itinerant science teacher or sharing your lab space with an itinerant teacher, make sure there is an ongoing system for sharing information about chemicals storage and safety issues and a day-to-day communication system to keep each other informed about special projects. Classroom plants and animals are at increased risk when science rooms are shared. It is important that all teachers sharing the space come to clear agreement on rules and procedures that will protect living organisms. (See Chapter 5, p. 55, for other factors to consider when choosing living things for the classroom.)

Backpack Facts

Students seem to be carrying more and more things to and from school—so much so that many backpacks are now equipped with wheels because their weight was causing back problems. Where to stow all the gear in school is becoming a more complex problem. By law, lockers are school property and can be searched for the general safety of the school. In most cases, items uncovered by such searches cannot be used as legal evidence. Student handbooks should notify students that searches of their lockers might be made.

Book bags and coats should remain in lockers or closets, not shoved under desks. In an emergency, items on the floor could block the exit or access to the eyewash. Items slung over the back of a chair can make the chair unstable and more likely to tip over.

If a middle school classroom has been relocated in a former elementary school, there may be cubbies in the classroom or storage spaces in desks. Neither of these are good storage spaces for students' personal items because they tend to accumulate dirt and junk. Work with the rest of your faculty to find ways of limiting the materials students carry from class to class.

Chemicals: Yours for Life

Did you know that, from the moment you purchase a chemical, your school is responsible for its disposal? Even if you turn it over to someone else, the fact is that if they stash it in the wrong place or dispose of it improperly, the chain of responsibility can bring the liability back to you and your school.

Imagine that you bought the heavy metal salt ammonium dichromate many years ago. It was once used for model volcanoes, a demonstration now considered unsafe and bad practice. But you have a large jar of ammonium dichromate, a known carcinogen, left. In a moment of weakness, you throw it in the trash. A student steals it from the dumpster and takes it home. Later, he dumps some of it in the garden where a cat gets into it and dies. You could be held responsible for the death of the cat. The chain of responsibility goes even farther. If your jar had made it to the local landfill a decade later, and the ammonium dichromate had contaminated a water source, you could be found negligent.

No Dumping

You cannot dispose of unwanted chemical and biological waste by simply pouring the materials down the sink, flushing them down the toilet, or dumping them into the trash.

Most of your unwanted materials can present hazards to the people who must handle them next and environmental hazards when they enter the waste stream or watershed. In large quantities, even common salt or plant fertilizer present serious environmental hazards. Some chemicals can be diluted or denatured and then discarded, but it is vital the directions for these procedures be followed to the letter.

▶ Be sure you read the MSDS when planning for proper disposal.
▶ Find out about relevant federal, state, and local regulations.
▶ If in doubt, consult with experts, such as the school facilities manager, district science supervisor, risk manager, hazardous waste coordinator, fire chief, and the U.S. Environmental Protection Agency.

Disposal is complex and can be very expensive. It can cost ten times more to dispose of an item than to purchase it. Look up the disposal issues before you purchase something. If it's hard to get rid of, don't buy it. Consider asking the school department to establish a contract with a reputable hazardous waste disposal company to remove hazardous wastes for all locations.

For chemicals you have now, look up the proper disposal methods or seek professional assistance. Although some materials can be diluted and put down the sink, remember that even the act of diluting some chemicals can be hazardous. Heavy metals such as cobalt, nickel, mercury, and lead should never be put into a water system or trash; neither should herbicides and pesticides.

Some Rules of Disposal

Organic matter must be sterilized or otherwise decontaminated before it is discarded. If you grow cultures, make sure they are sterilized before disposal. Flood agar plates with chlorine bleach for a minimum of five minutes. Experts do not recommend autoclaves because of other dangers. In any case, most middle schools don't have them. Kill molds with bleach or another disinfectant. Wrap terraria and animal bedding in plastic. You are responsible for the safety of everyone who handles the waste from your classroom, including custodial staff and trash collectors, as well as anyone who may use your classroom or preparation area after your activities.

Know the district policies and procedures for handling body fluids. (See "Standard Precautions," Chapter 10, p. 132.) Don't put anyone else at risk because they don't know what these are. Make sure all adults who might come into contact with body fluids are prepared to use Standard Precautions, and students should be given an abbreviated set of rules consistent with district and public health policy.

Some materials that are quite innocuous in small quantities can do extensive environmental damage when they go down the drain. One example is phosphates, found in strong detergents and plant foods. Significant quantities cause eutrophication in small bodies of water, resulting in algal growth. Animal droppings from cage bedding can have the same effect. Salt is another problem: Don't dump large quantities down the drain. Alert your students to safe disposal practices so they too can assist in protecting the environment.

Don't keep preserved specimens for more than a year. Molds grow even in preservatives. If you have formaldehyde or specimens preserved in formaldehyde from years ago, you cannot simply throw these materials away or dump the fluids down the sink. They are considered hazardous wastes and must be handled as such.

Where Do Things Go?

Students may not understand the cyclical nature of water and waste disposal. It's just gone! Consider having them trace a piece of trash from the classroom waste container to deposit in a landfill or follow a drop of water from the sink through the pipes to the sewage treatment facility and then back into local waters to organisms that may take it up and in time return it to us.

4

Even the disposal of equipment can be problematic. You need a special container for sharps such as blades, broken glass, and metal pieces. (See Chapter 10, "Use and Disposal of Sharps," p. 133.) Instruments containing mercury must be handled as hazardous waste. There are also special disposal procedures for electronic equipment, smoke detectors, and dry cells.

You May Need a Meeting

If this section has given you a headache because you've seen your storeroom described too accurately, it's time for a serious meeting with your school's administrator and your district maintenance director. Many teachers have inherited major storage and disposal problems and don't have the experience or funds to deal with them. At the meeting, concentrate on teamwork. Don't waste time and energy blaming former staff. Just plan for the future. You may need a special allocation of funds or even the services of a professional environmental hazard disposal firm to make your storage facility safe again. Once you have legally disposed of old chemicals and equipment, make sure they don't accumulate again.

Be Ruthless—Be Smart

Whether you are moving into renovated or new quarters, or just returning to old ones, each year you should take a hard look at your science inventory. Consider the program needs for the coming year, and keep very little else. Excellent middle school programs can function with limited storage, but it takes knowledge, care, and constant vigilance to make that happen.

It Seemed Great When I Did It...	A Better Middle School Alternative
Dissecting preserved specimens	Looking at muscles, bones, and cartilage in chicken wings or dissecting squid and fish in a sanitary way
Acid-base titration experiments	pH changes in aging soda pop
Phenolphthalein indicator for pH	Cabbage juice, beet juice, or tea as indicators of pH
Generation and testing of hydrogen	Investigating carbon dioxide generated by an antacid tablet
Violent exothermic chemical reactions	Heat of vaporization lab—a.k.a. watching water boil
Culturing environmental bacteria	Culturing yeast, surveying water for plankton to monitor water quality
Van de Graaff generators	Batteries and bulbs
Measuring the respiration of lab animals	Measuring the respiration of Elodea
Testing pond water with strong reagents	Testing pond water with probeware
Tasting phenylthiocarbamide (PTC) paper to test for a gene	Tasting cilantro to test for a gene
Killing insects with chloroform for collections	Field observations of insects
Chromatography requiring petroleum ether	Chromatography using water-soluble samples such as nonpermanent markers

Absence Makes the Lab Grow Sounder

Almost every teacher has experienced the problem: This year's budget is small, next year's may be nonexistent. You bought these washers and soda straws yourself. If you don't put them in the drawer, you may need to buy more next year. So the drawer fills up with three washers, four soda straws, two big alligator clips, a couple of dying batteries, and some spilled fish food.

Rule 1: Anything you haven't used in two years you probably don't need. And realistically, if you decide you do need it, you probably won't be able to find it and will buy it again.

Rule 2: Never accept hand-me-down chemicals and most specialized equipment from the high school, generous parents, or industry. High school reagent chemicals are far stronger than you need. Chemicals have shelf lives, and hand-me-downs may be of uncertain age and purity. The contents may have been contaminated by use. As the new owner, you will become responsible for disposal, which can be very costly.

Rule 3: Date your purchases. (See "Age Discrimination," p. 40.) If you have access to a chemical database software program, enter each purchase. At the very least, mark the date of purchase with indelible marker on the container and in the MSDS notebook.

Rule 4: Get a good storage guide for everything you buy.

Rule 5: If you can reduce the amount of stored items, do so. Scan worksheets to disk. Keep a Web address list rather than catalogs for supplies. Almost all companies have online catalogs now.

Rule 6: Never ignore a spill or a cloudy film on the inside of a chemical-storage cabinet. They are indicators the chemicals you have stored are reacting or decomposing, or containers may be broken or leaking. Never leave a jar with a rusted cap or crack in the cabinet. Spills and vapors are dangerous in themselves and even more so when two or more combine.

Your Second Home

Good storage and safe disposal procedures are even more important for you as an employee than for your students. Keep your second home as safe and secure as your primary residence. A stored chemical releasing a very low concentration of vapor may never be

4

Three True Storage Stories

▶ A middle school teacher accepted a sample of phosphorus from the secondary school and kept it in the storeroom with a collection of elements. It was stolen and carried home in a student's pocket. The student's body heat caused it to ignite, resulting in severe burns.

▶ A teacher in a high school shared by the middle school reported to police she thought some chemicals were missing, but couldn't be sure because the inventory was out of date. Investigation revealed that a middle school student had been gradually taking the chemicals home with the aim of making explosives.

▶ A middle school teacher moved into a renovated classroom where she found several rusty containers of chemicals, including one with the illegible notation "P...Acid." Fearing the container held picric acid, a school official had to call the bomb squad to remove the old bottle.

noticed by students but could trigger an allergic reaction or even worse in the classroom teacher who is in a class all day. Long-term exposure to heavy metals, formaldehyde, and other items found in some science classrooms has been associated with a variety of medical problems. In a middle school, you may also be responsible for shared spaces and environments. So many people may rotate through the rooms each day that extra care is needed.

The good news? It's possible—and better practice—to do a great, hands-on middle school science program with safe chemicals of low toxicity. Today's middle schoolers work so hard to look sophisticated and savvy, it's easy to forget that they need to explore simple phenomena. Experiences with familiar products can be memorable and are more appropriate developmentally for middle school students than mysterious alchemy. There is little justification for introducing high school materials into a program for early adolescents. It is also easier to maintain a safe, organized inventory with small amounts of less hazardous materials than to manage loaded shelves and cluttered storerooms.

THE SAVVY SCIENCE TEACHER

Mr. H teaches science systematically and has an exciting investigation-based program. His inventory is kept on 5" x 7" cards in a recipe box. Each has a reduced version of the MSDS warnings on the back. The cards are coded by color and symbol so he can quickly identify flammable chemicals, corrosives, and material that is quickly outdated.

Mr. H's locked cabinets are coded just like the cards. Each cabinet has the universal symbol for the chemical group on it in a corresponding color. The keys have a little colored tape on them so he can find them quickly.

The supply cabinet where equipment such as droppers, scissors, markers, and plastic dishes are kept is usually open. That's because the kids rotate responsibilities for cleaning and putting away those supplies. There's a picture of what the cabinet looks like full on the inside of the door.

Sure, the system took some time and effort to set up. But now that it's in place, adding new items is easy. As soon as Mr. H places his order, he has students help create the labels and index cards. Then when the items arrive, he just has to pull out the prepared information, complete the index card with the MSDS form, put the labels on, and put the item in its place.

Connections

▶ Flinn Scientific Catalog and website: *www.flinnsci.com*

▶ A good website for MSDSs for most chemicals: *hazard.com/msds*

▶ Links to most manufacturers' sites: *www.msdsprovider.net/Site/msdsprovider.nsf/about*

4

Lively Science
Live Organisms Are Worth the Work

If you teach and live in the same community, you may be meeting students and former students in informal situations—and finding out that the environment of your classroom has as much to do with what students remember as the lessons you formally teach. It happens all the time. You recognize the smile, the freckles, the wink. You hope the student will tell you about his college scholarship, or at least how inspired he was with your lectures. Then it comes: "Mom, I'd like you to meet the teacher that had that pair of gerbils and those plants that eat flies!"

5

The Perfect Time and Place

Middle school is the perfect setting for teaching life science. Students, besides being lively themselves, are intensely interested in their own bodies, reproduction, and other biological functions. Whether a school opts for an integrated program or a layer-cake approach, life science must be part of a good middle school science program.

Life Science Is about Living Things

Whether you have a major in science and teach in a dedicated science room or you are responsible for more than one discipline and depend on professional development work to learn science, you will find maintaining living organisms in your room and observing living organisms in the field are well worth the time and effort.

Observing and studying living organisms are critical to a good, strong program. Preserved specimens, computer simulations, photographs, and videos may be excellent supplements, but they should be used as enhancements to, rather than substitutes for, direct observation and work with living organisms. Maintaining living organisms in a safe and educationally sound manner requires serious effort. So it is important to remember just why it is worth extra work:

- Properly maintaining living things supports the development of respect for life.

- Observing the movement and behavior of living organisms encourages students to relate structure and function, stimulus and response.

- Learning how to maintain healthy living biosystems provides practical experience and adds to understanding of ecological concepts.

- Recognizing the requirements for keeping living things healthy teaches lessons about healthy living in the real world.

- Asking questions about living things provides the opportunity for students to explore complex concepts that cross academic disciplines.

Keeping live organisms in a classroom requires not only knowledge and preparation but also the proper equipment and space. Like selecting a pet, selecting a classroom organism requires a realistic appraisal of your situation. You should also check local district policy for restrictions or reporting requirements. How much space do you have? How much time can you give? How much control do you have? Is your classroom secure? How will plants and animals be maintained during weekends and vacations? Does an organism require a long-term commitment, perhaps many years? Are you willing to commit to a multi-year responsibility?

Is your room shared with other teachers? Do some students have special needs or allergies that would preclude certain types of organisms? Do you have students with behavioral problems that dictate additional precautions to ensure safety?

Resist the temptation to make headlines with your classroom pets. Some animals, such as larger mammals and exotic species, represent serious safety challenges with relatively low educational payoff. The table on the next page can help you make informed choices.

Greenhouses, Animal Rooms, Outdoor Facilities, and Other Special Places

Some middle schools are fortunate enough to have greenhouses and animal rooms as well as areas for outdoor planting and observation. These resources can enhance your curriculum. They can also give you the opportunity to involve your students in class or club activities that teach them the organizational and care responsibilities of maintaining the facilities and organisms in safe, clean, and useful condition.

Harnessing Energy

By asking your students to share in the responsibility for the care and maintenance of classroom biota, you may harness those pre-adolescent hormones to nurture, maintain, and defend the class plants and animals. You are likely to find that the more you involve your students, the more protective they become of the organisms and the facilities—peer pressure turned to positive outcomes.

Organism	Level of Care	Potential Problems
Plants	Low: need light and water, minimal care during vacations	▶ Molds on plants or in soil may be allergens; use sterilized potting soil ▶ Some plants are toxic
Aquarium fish, protists	Low: minimal care during vacations; constant temperature needed	▶ Risk of microbial infection ▶ Handwashing required ▶ Salmonella, mold, and other contamination from food and water containers ▶ Temperature controls may be required during vacations
Crustacea and snails	Moderate: simple foods, minimal care during vacations	▶ Moderate risk of bacterial contamination ▶ Exotic species may endanger the environment ▶ Some pinch
Insects	Moderate: cultures can become moldy; some care necessary during vacations	▶ Stings ▶ In cases of escape or release, exotic species may endanger the environment
Amphibians (tadpoles, frogs, salamanders)	Moderate: maintain reasonable temperatures	▶ Risk of microbial infection ▶ Salmonella, mold, and other contamination from food and water containers ▶ Many species are endangered; do not collect from the wild or release nonnative species
Reptiles (snakes, lizards, turtles)	High: many species require live food; intolerant of cold; require tight security	▶ Bites ▶ Salmonella, mold, and other contamination from food and water containers ▶ Escape and release risks are high
Rodents. rabbits, and other mammals	High: cannot be left unattended during vacations; require tight security	▶ Allergenic dander ▶ Odor and molds from droppings and bedding ▶ Bites and scratches ▶ Human disease carriers ▶ Escape and release risks are high

5

Your Classroom as an Ecosystem

Many teachers maintain live cultures—plants and animals that are attractive, highly motivating, and models of good and humane care and thoughtful and responsible management. Unfortunately, other classroom environments resemble unmanaged landfills with menageries that are poorly cared for and pose risks to both the organisms and the humans that occupy the room.

The key difference lies in thought, preparation, and long-term commitment. Think of your classroom as a model ecosystem. In addition to understanding fully the care requirements of any individual organism you bring to your classroom, think about the whole classroom environment, including allergenic and disease hazards the organisms can pose to each other and to the human inhabitants.

Consider the following as you build or modify your classroom ecosystem:

▶ Are there potentially allergenic dander, molds, or materials present in animals, food, and bedding, in plant and potting material, in aquaria and other aquatic environments?

▶ Can you sufficiently monitor and control the behavior of your students—and others who use your room—to ensure that the organisms will not be harmed or subject to unauthorized release?

▶ Do you have a plan to ensure that the organisms are fed and watered and environments cleaned as frequently as health and sanitation require—even when you are absent?

▶ Do you have a complete plan for caring safely for organisms during weekends and vacations?

▶ Have you taken steps to prevent unwanted procreation of classroom animals? Should they arrive, what would you do with the progeny?

▶ Do you have the right cages, terraria, and aquaria? Are they secure?

▶ Do you have convenient access to water and sinks to facilitate washing and cleaning? Are hand-washing sinks close to places where organisms are touched and handled?

▶ What will happen to the organisms at the end of the school year?

▶ Are you prepared to deal with the death of a classroom animal?

YEAR-ROUND ALLERGY SEASON

For a variety of reasons, allergies and sensitivity to environmental contaminants are becoming more and more common. Both adults and students can react to organisms and materials that had never been a problem because sensitivity can build up from multiple exposures or because heightened sensitivity to all materials might be induced by exposure to contaminants in environments outside the classroom. Although some sensitivities may be specifically identified in individual education plans (IEPs) and other notes in students' records, many students and their parents may not even be aware of allergies to organisms and materials you are considering. For this reason, avoid organisms known to create problems and be particularly alert to any signs of sensitivity—sneezes, runny noses, itches, rashes, headaches, increased illness or absences—when you bring any new organism or material to your classroom.

Pick a Critter

Let's take a closer look at some of the species commonly chosen for classroom culture. Remember, regardless of the species you choose, do not release nonnative species to the natural environment. See "Escape and Release," p. 67.

Bacteria

Some textbooks still suggest that students culture and study environmental bacteria. Outdated texts may even suggest that students culture their own bacteria by touching agar plates or culturing scrapings from the mouth or under the fingernails. This should never be done. Infectious *streptococci* and *staphylococci* are indigenous to the population in your classroom. Although a normal immune system can withstand the challenge from small amounts of bacteria, exposure to the millions or billions of bacteria in a broken or carelessly handled culture dish can quickly overwhelm the body's immune mechanisms, resulting in serious infection and disease. You could produce a major strep or staph outbreak with disastrous results.

SCI LINKS.
THE WORLD'S A CLICK AWAY

Topic: bacteria
Go to: *www.scilinks.org*
Code: SML57

At the middle school level, unless you are well trained and have the appropriate facilities, even culturing vendor-supplied bacteria on agar plates is not recommended because you risk accidental contamination with human infectious agents. This is one topic for which technology—photos and video clips—is preferred to an actual classroom culture.

A standard tool of bacteriology, the autoclave, can be very dangerous if not used appropriately, and the common substitute, the pressure cooker, can become a bomb, releasing superheated steam. They are not recommended at the middle school level, and neither are exercises that require them.

If you wish to show bacterial cultures, we strongly suggest you buy stock cultures and make sure each container is unbreakable, completely sealed, and has never been opened. Here are a number of safer and equally exciting options for teaching microbiology:

▶ For survey studies, use commercially available closed systems. These systems can be inoculated but then are permanently closed to prevent exposure and contamination.

▶ You can test for bacterial presence and activity without multiplying the bacteria. Over-the-counter test strips from pharmacies—such as UTI (urinary tract infection) test strips—detect the byproducts of bacterial action rather than the bacteria itself.

▶ For demonstrations of microbial metabolism, consider yeast or yogurt-forming bacteria.

▶ Instead of culturing soil bacteria, survey the indicators or products of microbial presence in the soil such as pH, color, and texture.

▶ Test for the effects of bacterial action by using an indicator like bromthymol blue that measures pH changes from carbon dioxide.

Serratia marcescens

Although the microbe *Serratia marcescens* was once recommended for life science activities, it has been found to be pathogenic for some people and should not be used for middle school science activities.

Protists

Living, moving, and dividing *Amoebae, Paramecia,* and *Euglena* are diverse in form and fascinating to observe. These protists can be seen with stereoscopes or compound microscopes with relatively low magnification. A microprojector or video attachment for your microscope is an ideal tool to engage the entire class in studying pond water. Observation of protists in a water sample can reveal a lot about the environmental health of a pond or other water source.

SCI*LINKS.*
THE WORLD'S A CLICK AWAY

Topic: protista
Go to: www.scilinks.org
Code: SML58

When collecting water samples from the environment, be very careful about selecting your water source. Do not ask students to collect water samples unsupervised or on their own because of risk of drowning or infection. What a student may consider "pond water" could be the top of a neighbor's cesspool, contaminated farm run-off in a drainage ditch, or chemical drainage from an upstream manufacturing facility. Potentially polluted samples, including common ditch and runoff water, require special handling. Keep in mind the possibility that toxins or heavy metals may be present. When in doubt, assume water is polluted and potentially dangerous. If unpolluted pond water is unavailable, substitute a hay infusion or commercially prepared sample.

Review aseptic technique. Provide nonlatex gloves and eye protection when students are studying water samples. Have a disposal plan for sampled water, and remind students to wash their hands immediately following the activity and to never eat in the classroom.

HAND-WASHING DEMONSTRATION

5

Divide students into small groups that can play a simple card game such as hearts. Apply a small amount of body glitter to the hands of one student in each group. Pause after several minutes of play to check the spread of the glitter, the "pathogen." After playing the game, have the students wash their hands thoroughly and check how carefully the hand washing must be done to ensure that no glitter remains. The lesson should convince students that hand washing is very important.

As with all activities, test your procedures beforehand to make sure the amount of glitter you use will work effectively.

Studying protists presents a good opportunity to remind students about the importance of hygiene, hand washing, and modern methods of water treatment. Some of the most dangerous waterborne diseases are caused by protists. *Cryptosporidium parvum,* found in water fountains and pools, is a parasite that causes diarrhea. Other protists cause intestinal diseases such as dysentery. These protists are found not only in natural settings but also in ordinary classroom plumbing fixtures, such as the eyewash or rubber faucet extenders. Flush out these water sources regularly, and do not drink water from them.

Fungi

The kingdom Fungi includes molds, mildews, yeast, and mushrooms. Many are unwanted visitors in classrooms because of their persistence and tendency to cause allergic reactions. The reproductive spores are the most troublesome. Don't culture fungi, except for mushrooms and yeast.

MOLDS AND MILDEW—GUESTS THAT STAY FOREVER

Molds and mildew, once established, are almost impossible to remove. They are harbored in carpeting and mats, animal bedding and litter, germinating seeds, plant and soils taken directly from the outside, and artifacts in the deep dark reaches of student cubbies, desks, and lockers. Mold spores are easily airborne and carried to air ducts and filters where they multiply and further spread throughout the building. Ridding classrooms and buildings of these persistent allergens can be very expensive.

Rather than deliberately culturing molds, engage your students in a hunt for sources of persistent molds and mildew at home and in school. Identify items for disposal before molds can grow, and arrange for the safe removal of already-contaminated items.

Do not let students bring wild mushrooms into the classroom; some are poisonous even to the touch, and some can provoke dangerous allergic reactions. Grocery stores provide varieties of mushroom specimens that are generally safer. Commercial systems for culturing classroom mushrooms are educational and easy, but inform your students and their parents well in advance of any activity involving mushrooms, so you can be alerted to students who might be allergic to the culture.

When you show molds to students, keep the exercise short, specific, and contained. You can grow bread mold on homemade white bread—most commercially produced breads are made with mold inhibitors—or on old fruit, but keep the specimens in sealed containers when showing them. Immediately after the activity, disinfect the samples with a 10% bleach solution and follow with proper disposal in a garbage disposal or sealed bag. Make sure custodians and service personnel are never exposed to discarded live cultures.

SCI*LINKS.
THE WORLD'S A CLICK AWAY

Topic: Fungi
Go to: *www.scilinks.org*
Code: SML60

Yeasts make excellent subjects for life-science experiments. Baker's yeast is inexpensive and available in grocery stores. It is easily cultured in a sterile molasses-water solution. If you are preparing a yeast product for eventual consumption, remember to do it in a kitchen, cafeteria, or home economics room—not in areas designated for science activities.

Plants

Plants are attractive, easy to maintain, and provide valuable, timely lessons. But be cautious with some areas:

Topic: toxic plants
Go to: *www.scilinks.org*
Code: SML61

▶ Some common plants or parts of plants are toxic if eaten, such as alamanda, oleander, hemlock, poinsettias, dieffenbachia, and holly berries.

▶ Some plants with edible parts have parts that are inedible and quite toxic, such as potato leaves, rhubarb leaves, and walnut husks.

▶ Some plants can cause itching and blistering on contact. The most common of these are members of the *Rhus* family, commonly known as poison ivy, poison oak, and poison sumac.

▶ Some plants produce toxic fumes when burned. These include the *Rhus* plants and oleander. Be certain to avoid burning these materials to get rid of them, or using them as kindling or firewood.

Be explicit. Warn your students not to taste any plants or parts of plants in your classroom, at field sites, or even in their home gardens or yards unless the plants have been specifically grown for food—and even then they should taste only the edible parts. Explain to them that allergic reactions can result from multiple exposures. Students who claim they have handled poison ivy with no ill effect can develop serious sensitivity.

Be aware that unwanted molds can grow along with seeds or on plant potting soil. Treat seeds with a solution of 1% chlorine bleach for an hour before using them for science activities. Use sterilized potting soil indoors, not soil dug up from outside. Don't keep too many plants: You risk greater likelihood of mold growth and plant diseases when plants are too closely spaced.

If you have access to a schoolyard nature area or garden, try to cultivate native plants rather than risk bringing in plants that do not belong in your local environment or that compete with native species. Remind students to wash their hands after planting and gardening.

Some Common Toxic Plants

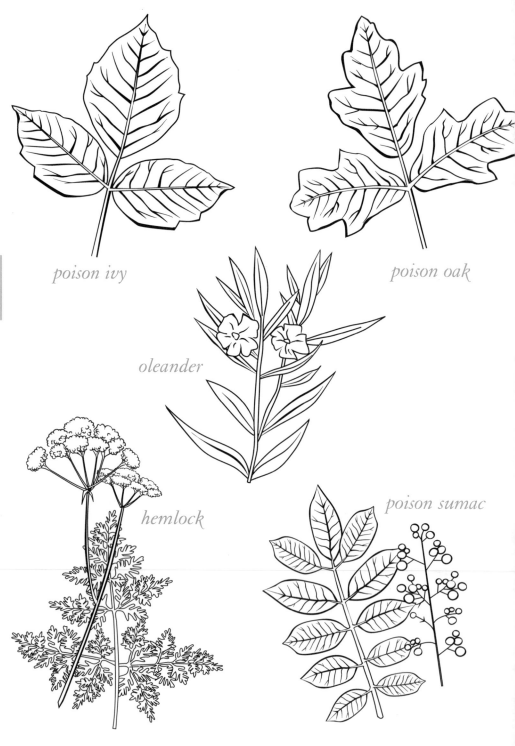

poison ivy

poison oak

oleander

hemlock

poison sumac

5

Invertebrates

For stimulus-response and life-cycle studies, invertebrates make excellent choices. They are relatively easy to maintain, they're usually inexpensive, and they reproduce quickly. Because invertebrate metabolism is different from ours, they are less likely to carry diseases that can spread to humans.

Another advantage of invertebrates is that they are plentiful: The vast majority of animal species do not have backbones. Arthropods such as insects, spiders, and crustaceans are invertebrates with external skeletons. Populations of fruit flies, mealworms, pill bugs, ants, and dermestid beetles can be raised easily in jars or small terraria. *Daphnia* and brine shrimp are aquatic invertebrates barely visible to the eye, but their heartbeats can be studied under various conditions with a low-power stereo "dissecting" microscope. Giant cockroaches and hermit crabs don't take up much space, and their food is usually easy to obtain: dried fruit, plants, and grains.

Although invertebrates are small and relatively easy to care for, some are hazards and should not be collected or cultured. The main danger from insects is stinging. The bites of bees, wasps, and fire ants can be very painful and sometimes fatal. You may have students so allergic that a prescribed EpiPen injection is maintained for them in the office, but others also can react severely and unexpectedly. Don't take the chance. (See "First Aid" in Chapter 10, page 132, for more on using an EpiPen.)

Crabs can pinch, although the pinch may be more frightening than the actual injury inflicted. Be mindful of molds in insect terraria. Those dried bananas and apples fed to invertebrates can breed allergenic molds.

If you have collected invertebrates from an outdoor habitat, try to return the organisms following observations. If you cannot return them to their original habitat, freeze-kill them before disposal.

Fish

Aquarium fish are common and convenient classroom organisms. They can be maintained safely with a few commonsense precautions. Like all classroom animals, fish should come from a reputable dealer. You do not want exotic species brought directly from another country. Resist the temptation to bring excitement into your classroom in the form of notorious species such as piranhas, large Oscar fish, and live sharks—the risk and liability are not justifiable.

Regular cleaning and maintenance of the aquarium are necessary. Remind students about hand washing. Remember also that heat and air conditioning in your building may be turned off overnight or during weekends and extended vacations.

SCI*LINKS*.
THE WORLD'S A CLICK AWAY

Topic: invertebrates
Go to: www.scilinks.org
Code: SML63

Aquaria residents may not be able to survive the temperature change.

Amphibians

Metamorphoses of amphibians can make interesting long-term observations for your students. Care for tadpoles is similar to that for fish. Toads and salamanders may be kept in terraria. However, be aware that many of these species are endangered. Do not take organisms from the wild or release nonnative species. A few amphibians in the southern United States are venomous, so know your species.

Reptiles

Many teachers find that small reptiles are convenient classroom pets because they provide a lot of opportunities for observation and can tolerate infrequent feedings. But even small reptiles require special attention to security and other precautions.

Nonvenomous snakes may bite. Even some species—such as garter snakes—that people don't expect to bite, do. Nonvenomous snakes also may have secretions that cause serious effects in sensitive people. Small lizards and geckos can be good substitutes, but a few do bite. Iguanas require special care and are not recommended. You may want to maintain a culture of live crickets as food for some reptiles.

Reptiles do not generate their own heat or self-regulate body temperature as mammals do, so you must be particularly careful to ensure the reptile environment is steadily maintained at the proper temperature. You may have to use heat lamps and other devices. Keep combustibles away from the heat lamps, and make sure the outlet you use is rated to carry the amperage required.

Snakes and lizards seem to attract theft and vandalism more than many other classroom objects and have an uncanny ability to escape, so take steps to secure these animals. Large snakes, such as boa constrictors, can also pose a strangulation hazard to smaller animals, including small humans.

Snake Escape!

Even when secured carefully, snakes have a high rate of escape. If your snake does escape, it will most likely head for the heating system—ducts, blowers, and unit ventilators—where it can find warmth and entry to spaces in and behind the walls.

You can try to lure the escapee back out into the open by placing an incandescent or heat lamp close to the ducts or grills and leaving the lamp turned on during evening hours when the room is unoccupied. Be sure the electric receptacle can carry sufficient amperage for the lamp and no papers or other combustible items are nearby. Three-foot boas have been known to disappear for more than two weeks and then turn up two floors below basking in a pool of morning sunshine on a student's desk.

Birds

Birds bred by legitimate breeders are generally free from diseases that are zoonotic—transmittable to humans. But every year a few cases are reported of disease transmitted by birds brought into the country illegally. Duck and goose droppings and unsterilized owl pellets may also carry agents infectious to humans. Buy commercial owl pellets: Don't dissect those you find.

Birds can bite and scratch; their cages can become moldy or insect-infested. However, the chief danger in keeping birds is to the animals themselves—they are fragile and easily disturbed. Birds need a calm environment with a constant temperature.

Students may bring living things to the science teacher spontaneously—especially injured animals. Try to prevent or discourage this practice by emphasizing the need to maintain living creatures in their natural habitat. Do not attempt to nurse wild birds or animals in your classroom. This could pose dangers to you and the students. For most animals, a special permit is required. If students report a sick animal, call for expert help from the local animal control officer, the humane society, and agencies specializing in rescuing wild animals.

Mammals

Resist the lure of big eyes and a furry body unless you are very sure you have a healthy, calm animal and you are ready for a lot of work. Mammals, particu-

Call of the Wild

Do not bring wild or feral animals—dead or alive—into your classroom. They may

- be sick, diseased, or hurt
- carry a variety of infectious agents
- be protected by federal, state, and local regulations
- require special licensing
- be much more aggressive than domesticated animals

Further problems:

- Mammals can carry zoonotic diseases such as rabies, leptospirosis (rabbits), hantavirus, and even plague (rodents).
- Birds may carry ticks and other infectious agents.
- Parasites may spread to domestic animals and humans.

larly larger ones, are probably the most difficult and demanding of classroom pets. Because other mammals bear a close species relationship to humans, they also carry more human infectious diseases.

If you have enough time, space, and cleanup facilities, healthy gerbils or white mice make good classroom mammals. With more than one of a kind, avoid an exploding population by making sure they are the same sex. Purchase animals from a reputable pet store to ensure they do not carry disease. Get animals accustomed to being handled by working with them yourself before you allow students near them.

GERBILS

Of all the mammals you might consider, gerbils are one of the best choices. If you have enough space and are prepared for the additional work, they can provide interesting observational studies for your middle school students. Although most small mammals are nocturnal, gerbils are often active during daylight hours. And because they are desert animals, they secrete relatively less urine than other rodents.

They are communal animals. You will find they are most interesting to observe when you keep two or more together. To avoid procreation, make sure the gerbils are the same sex. To avoid territorial disputes, introduce all of them to the common environment at the same time.

Rather than purchase expensive prefabricated gerbilaria, you and your students should be able to find instructions for making fine gerbil residences from abandoned leaky aquaria or hardware cloth, galvanized trash can lids and canning jars.

Rabbits, Hamsters, and Guinea Pigs

Rabbits, hamsters, and guinea pigs are less reliable pets. When frightened, they are prone to scratch and bite. Even when purchased from reliable sources, they often carry or contract diseases.

Mammals have a protein dander under their skin that is a strong allergen to many students. Rabbits and guinea pigs cause the biggest problem. Because this protein cannot be washed or vacuumed away and may remain in a classroom for many years after the animal has been removed, keeping mammals in a carpeted classroom is not recommended.

Escape and Release

An animal AWOL from your classroom does not make for happy colleagues or friendly news stories. Your principal does not want to pay for exterminating the building to rid it of a colony of rodents born to the ones released when you left your classroom unlocked. Nor would the music teacher be happy to discover your garter snake wrapped around the tuba in his instrument closet. Additionally, middle school students can get very emotional at the loss or death of a classroom pet. Make sure you are prepared to protect your classroom organisms from escape or deliberate release.

Some teachers culture fruit flies for observation and genetic activities, but keeping them contained can be a challenge. Be particularly mindful of inadvertently releasing them. Your colleagues and cafeteria workers would not appreciate your experimental critters in their lunches.

You should also avoid emulating the scientist who tried to start a silk industry and ended up introducing the gypsy moth to the United States. There are serious environmental consequences when exotic—nonnative—animals and plants are introduced to local ecosystems. Someone loved zebra mussels and English sparrows in their original homes, but in environments without natural predators they have multiplied unchecked. Kudzu, purple loosestrife, and Russian thistle are all plants that fit well in their native habitats but are wreaking havoc in new places. So, too, plants or seeds brought back from a student's vacation can cause serious problems at home.

One of the most common examples of misplaced eco-enthusiasm is releasing butterflies. Commercial butterfly farms have become sources of disease, spread across the country by well-intentioned teachers and newlyweds. Misplaced butterflies have confused migration and complicated gene pools, endangering native species. If you raise butterflies, purchase only a few from a reputable source and limit your butterfly garden to your schoolyard.

Feeding mallard ducks and Canada geese or hatching the eggs of wild species can domesticate them to such an extent they don't take their normal fall trips south. Before you begin culturing an organism in your classroom, think about what you will do with it when the activity or the school year comes to an end.

A Home of Their Own

Observing the behavior of living organisms in their own habitats provides rich science experiences. As you

> ## Rules for the Nature Center
> - Observe quietly, and do not touch or disturb wild animals.
> - Report all scratches, bites, or stings.
> - Do not taste or eat plants or other materials.
> - Do not approach or touch sick or injured animals, animal parts, or carcasses.
> - Wash hands after outdoor activities.

5

plan for safe and sensitive experiences with organisms, don't forget the schoolyard. Nature areas, gardens, and bird and animal feeders can attract species for a closer look. Even in urban settings, look for mini-biomes in tree pits, parks, and cracks and crevices in sidewalks and buildings.

Culture native plants and attract native wildlife to school nature centers. As you plan, ensure handicap accessibility and security. A good fence may be needed to keep out unwanted intruders on foot and in vehicles.

Students as Living Laboratories

Health and anatomy lessons are especially suitable at the middle school level. Students can participate in many safe observational activities as subjects as well as observers. Take a few basic precautions:

▶ Students can look at their own skin or hair with appropriate precautions. Make sure each student works only with samples from himself or herself and no one else. Use disposable slides. If they are glass—which is not recommended—give specific instructions for safe handling. Instruct students to place slides and stirrers in 10% bleach disinfectant immediately after use—not at the end of the activity—to prevent communicating infectious agents. Provide a specific disposal plan for the slides and stirrers.

▶ Before beginning any studies that involve exercise or other means of increasing a student's heart rate, make sure you inform students and parents of the activity and receive written confirmation that they have been informed and give their permission. Check with the school nurse, IEPs, and other records for health problems that may preclude or require modifying the activity. Never schedule these activities during hot and humid weather, and warn students to stop immediately if they sense any discomfort.

▶ Use prepared amylase, not saliva, to hydrolyze starch. Saliva presents too much risk of infection.

▶ Do not collect, type, test, or otherwise use human blood. If your curriculum requires a blood-typing demonstration, use purchased kits with synthetic antigens. It is not just using your own or your students' blood that presents a risk. The

Heart Rate Studies and the Adolescent Spirit

Heart-rate studies are designed to observe and measure change rather than to determine a maximum or sustained elevated rate. Middle school students are particularly geared toward pushing things beyond their limits and cannot be counted on to understand control and moderation. You must not only instruct your students carefully about working only enough to detect change, but you also must monitor them throughout the activity to ensure moderation.

older antigens that were sold in blood-test kits were prepared from untested blood purchased "on the street" and could present hepatitis and HIV risks.

▶ If you use straws for respiration experiments or swabs for taste experiments, do not reuse any material that has been touched by human body fluids. Have a disposal plan, and instruct students to discard contaminated items immediately in a place where the custodian will not be infected.

▶ Do not use pins or any other sharp implement for sensory nerve assays. Use coffee stirrers or hair roller picks, and properly dispose of all used items.

▶ Consider all blood and body fluids to be infectious, and refer to Chapter 10, p. 132, for a discussion of Standard Precautions.

The Dissection Dilemma

During the past decade, dissection activities below the secondary level have become controversial. There are many arguments pro and con, some related to personal and environmental safety and some to ethics and pedagogy:

▶ Dissection specimens have historically been taken from the wild, depleting natural populations.

▶ Large or unruly classes may not be under sufficient control to allow students to use sharp instruments.

▶ Dissection preservatives are toxic and often allergenic.

▶ Some middle school students may not be emotionally mature enough to handle a dissection experience.

▶ Traditional dissection lessons have focused too much on simple identification and rote memory.

On the other hand, proponents of the dissection experience argue that students can learn a lot with carefully supervised dissections structured around inquiry questions rather than just finding and naming parts. If you decide your students are ready for a well-crafted dissection experience, exercise the following precautions:

▶ In using unpreserved food material, be sure to follow careful hand-washing and cleanup procedures to prevent transmitting food-borne diseases such as *salmonella* and *e. coli*. In all other cases, use only material obtained from a reputable science supply house.

▶ Do not bring the body of a dead feral animal into a classroom. Do not dissect roadkill or shelter animals. Dead animals can spread viral and bacterial diseases even many days after they die. Dead animals also have persistent ticks, molds, and other parasites.

Housecleaning in Life Science

A life science classroom has special cleaning requirements:

▶ Make sure you have a supply of liquid soap, paper towels, and hot water for hand washing and hygiene. Or try the newer alcohol hand-cleaning gels.

▶ Clean desks and counters with soap and bleach disinfectant following life science activities.

▶ Remember, stains *stain*. Use minimal quantities and learn how to neutrialize spills. Keep all stains secure so students don't use them for tattoos. Check toxicity and hazards of biological stains. Some may be carcinogenic or teratogenic. Do not use hematoxylin, safranin, methyl red or methyl orange (carcinogens).

▶ Designate a disposal container for biological waste.

▶ Using disinfectants and pesticides in school buildings is now covered by federal regulations. Be sure you know and conform to the latest rulings.

▶ Use heat-resistant gloves or mitts for handling hot labware. Have nonlatex gloves for cleaning spills and stains and handling preserved specimens.

▶ Do not collect specimens from the field. Local populations, especially amphibians, have been depleted by otherwise well-meaning science activities.

▶ Plan to monitor students closely and instruct them specifically on the use of sharp instruments and cutting tools.

▶ Prepare specific containers and procedures for discarding disposable sharps and safely cleaning reusable sharp instruments. (See Chapter 10, "Use and Disposal of Sharps," p. 133.)

▶ Prepare specific containers for proper disposal of biological waste. Do not dump preservatives and preserved specimens down the drain.

▶ Require the use of sanitized eye protection and nonlatex (vinyl) gloves by everyone participating in a dissection activity.

▶ Treat all preservatives and preserved specimens as corrosive, toxic, and hazardous. Do not allow students access to stock containers containing preservative fluids. Use low toxicity preservatives, and keep the material safety data sheet (MSDS) out and available. Do not keep specimens and solutions from year to year because molds can grow even on preserved specimens.

A traditional activity no longer considered safe is preparing skeletons from found carcasses (often dermestid beetles). The preceding information explains why roadkill and fallen animals should not be brought into the school. If you find or prepare skeletons yourself, use nonlatex gloves at all times and treat bones with bleach before bringing them to the classroom.

In the Supply Closet

Life science activities can involve as many toxic materials and chemicals as do chemistry activities. As

Topic: animal experiments
Go to: *www.scilinks.org*
Code: SML70

5

ETHICAL RESPONSIBILITY

▶ If your science program entails using vertebrates, begin discussions with your students about the role of living organisms in science. If you keep living vertebrates, then class discussion of good and humane care should accompany the introduction of the animals.

▶ At the middle school level, try to plan activities that involve observation of normal animal behavior before embarking on activities that change or challenge normal behavior.

▶ If you are required or intend to include dissection—other than of specimens ordinarily considered to be food—in your program, consider a brief but serious discussion that reminds students a living organism will be sacrificed for the activity.

▶ There may be students in your class whose conscience, religion, or sensitivity makes them unwilling to work with sacrificed animals. If so, you need to provide a meaningful alternative activity to allow those students to achieve the same educational goals, preferably at the same time as their peers. Your leadership in respecting these students' concerns serves as a model for the rest of your students. In many state and local jurisdictions, alternative activities may be required by regulation or ordinance.

5

our understanding of toxicity increases, we must eliminate many chemicals once commonly used. If you inherited any of the following chemicals from prior or upper-grade teachers, contact a reliable disposal firm—you need to get them out of your room, but you cannot dump them down the drain or in the trash:

▶ Toluene and benzene—used for embedding samples.

▶ Ethers and chloroform—used for chromatography or for anesthetizing insects.

▶ Heavy metals—such as elemental mercury or chromium compounds commonly found in stains and metallic salts.

▶ Colchicine—once used for mitosis slides.

▶ Carbon tetrachloride—a once commonly used solvent.

▶ Biological stains—hematoxylin, safranin, methyl red, methyl orange.

Formaldehyde

Formaldehyde solution—also called formalin—has been replaced largely by newer, less odorous, and less toxic preservatives with a variety of trade names. However, most still contain formaldehyde, albeit in lesser concentrations and mixed with other ingredients. Treat all specimen preservatives as though they contain formaldehyde, particularly if you or your students are sensitive to materials of this type.

The Flinn Scientific Catalog/Reference Manual contains a good discussion of the issue.

Although some firms still pack specimens in formaldehyde, it is not recommended. Because prolonged exposure to this chemical can cause cancer, ask for a substitute preservative. (See box, left.)

For other reagents, refer to storage rules in Chapter 4, p. 39, and recommendations in Appendix A, p. 165, "Chemicals to Go." Make sure the storeroom is secure, and the sections for combustibles, corrosives, and organics are separate.

You may spend more money, but you are better off ordering chemicals in the strength you need rather than in more concentrated forms for later dilution. Order only what you need for one year—programs may change and chemicals may decompose or become contaminated.

Pets from Home

Qualitative and quantitative behavioral studies are important activities to include in your life science curriculum. You can teach students a great deal by introducing them to methods for observing their own pets at home. But be cautious about inviting your students to bring their pets to school. They may get nervous and scratch or bite when brought into your classroom.

If a pet will be brought to school, make sure it has been properly cared for and all its required veterinary inoculations are current. Do not permit a visit from any animal that has had any episodes of biting or aggressive behavior. Invite only one pet at a time. Dogs and other domesticated animals that are very gentle with humans in their home setting can become extremely aggressive in a strange setting with their owner surrounded by strangers or other animals.

Sensitive Topics in the Life Science Curriculum

Some topics in life science curricula may not pose safety hazards, but do raise issues of sensitivity and liability. We include them to raise your awareness of potential controversy.

It's Not All in the Genes

Some middle school curricula include genetic activities that direct students to survey themselves and family members for a variety of genetic traits. Bear in mind that today's families include many members not genetically related—adopted children, half-siblings, children from previous unions—some of whose relationships may not be known to your student. You need to be sensitive to the possibility of inadvertently exposing a relationship that the parents or guardians of your student have chosen not to share. The pre-adolescent years may find some adopted children becoming concerned about relations with their adoptive parents, their biological parents, and other circumstances of their adoption. Think about these possibilities beforehand, and consider how to handle situations that may arise.

Evolution

The National Science Teachers Association has taken a strong stand advocating teaching evolution as an important element of the life sciences. This position is reinforced in national and state curriculum benchmarks and frameworks. Unfortunately, in some states and localities, opponents of this position continue to use a variety of legal and political means to block instruction on evolution or include nonscience topics in conjunction with evolutionary theory.

Topic: evolution in the science classroom
Go to: *www.scilinks.org*
Code: SML73

You are best protected by being thoroughly familiar with the nationally recognized standards and your state and local curriculum requirements as well as the professional organizations available to support you. It is best not to engage in this battle alone.

Sex Education

Middle school science teachers often double as health teachers, and health topics are often an integral part of science curricula. Discussions of human reproduction, human sexuality, and sexually transmitted diseases (STDs) are often part of the curriculum. Make sure you know your local district policy requirements on notifying parents and on whether parents and guardians have the right to exclude their children from sex education sessions. If parents do have the right to withdraw their children during discussions of certain topics, you owe it to the student to ensure the decision and the student are treated respectfully not only by you but also by the student's peers.

THE SAVVY SCIENCE TEACHER

Ms. K begins her classroom cultures by asking groups of students to research the habitat needs of simple, inexpensive animals—mealworms, guppies, crickets, and Daphnia—all relatively easy to culture. Sometimes she selects invertebrates available in a local bait shop for loose change.

Once a group of students have demonstrated they know how to maintain their organism, they are given the responsibility of culture for a limited period of time. During that time, they make quantitative observations of the living organism—the studies are called "ethograms"—and produce a report or class presentation. By October, Ms. K's students have developed a display of their creatures that is shared with elementary students.

5

Modern Alchemy
Safer Teaching with Chemistry

Gee, you don't look like the Nutty Professor, Merlin the Magician, or Snow White's stepmother complete with bubbling cauldron. Could you really be a chemist? The mad scientists may be gone from modern research and industry, but they still live on in movies, DVDs, and MTV. Thank Alan Alda and television's Scientific American Frontiers for giving us some alternative images and a fighting chance to compete.

The Magic of Chemistry

From making mud pies in a sandbox to messing with a magic set and sending secret messages with markers that produce invisible writing, chemistry engages students' passions for mixing things together and producing surprising results. With each young adolescent's maturing body comes a mind that can't be quenched—and a curiosity that goes beyond the limits of caution. Middle schoolers want to dare higher mountains and investigate more mysteries as each day goes on. Their newfound reasoning skills allow them to explore concepts about the unseen—atoms, molecules, and forces—that were only hazy notions to their younger selves. Their energy makes it all the more important you teach not only chemistry but also caution. Your job is to preserve their natural curiosity and willingness to observe while ensuring the observed phenomenon does no harm—no small task in today's environment. The good news is that basic chemistry concepts can be taught with safe and fascinating activities. In doing so, we also arm students with the knowledge they need to recognize the dangers of "just messing around" with formulas, recipes, and chemicals.

Common Chemistry Misconceptions

- Atoms and molecules are just a bit smaller than a tiny grain of sand.
- Atoms are solid (rather than mostly empty space).
- An atom resembles the solar system with protons and neutrons in the center like the sun and electrons cruising around in orbits like planets.
- Chemical reactions always result in explosions.
- When chemicals are mixed together they always get hotter.

6

The best chemical explorations can also be the safest. You can provide your students with many opportunities to observe chemical phenomena that, by their very simplicity, are fascinating, as well as safe. Allow middle school students to control and manipulate chemical change. Then extend the logic to apply to real world situations.

Taking a cue from Content Standard B in *National Science Education Standards* (NRC 1996), consider experiences for your students in "properties and changes of properties in matter" and "transfer of energy."

For the property Standard you can work with:

▶ properties of elements and compounds

▶ physical changes like phase changes, solubility

▶ chemical changes—simple reactions which fall into recognizeable patterns

For the energy Standard, try:

▶ microscale, controlled exothermic and endothermic reactions

▶ photosynthesis and respiration

All can be done safely.

Stay Close to Home

Students learn best when the lessons are rooted in the familiar. Middle school students have wider experiences than elementary youngsters, so there are many more ways to connect lessons to the chemicals they see in their homes and immediate environment. Curriculum developers often use the word "authentic" to describe such experiences.

When you are searching for hands-on experiences for students, begin in the home, kitchen, or grocery store. However, do not ask students to bring chemicals to school or to experiment with chemicals at home. Every home has chemicals that are toxic, caustic, combustible, reactive, or otherwise hazardous. You cannot be certain of the selection, the contents, and the packaging of the materials your students may be finding at home. Nor do you want to

Chemistry from the Cupboard

▶ When doing acid and base studies, begin with carbonated beverages, lemon juice, vinegar, liquid hand soap, and baking soda. Middle schoolers can handle some diluted acids and bases, but should practice with milder materials first.

▶ For indicators, use tea, beet juice, or red cabbage juice rather than phenolphthalein or bromthymol blue. Use electronic probes for continuous recording of pH.

▶ For organic molecules, use foods such as sugars and starches. But do not permit eating in the classroom laboratory.

▶ To demonstrate solubility, use table salt, Epsom salts, sugar, starch, and powdered drink mixes.

▶ Pollution studies can be carried out with silt, clay, powdered milk, or ice-melt salts rather than more toxic materials.

6

take the responsibility for possible misuse of those items in transit from home to your classroom.

Every chemical that comes into the classroom should be accompanied with a material safety data sheet (MSDS). (For a detailed explanation of these documents, see Chapter 4, "Material Safety Data Sheets," p. 41.)

Small Is Better

Even when you are using familiar substances, accidents can occur. In the most disciplined room, there may be a student who sneaks a taste of something. Using the smallest possible quantity of a reagent is not only good practice but also encourages students to work carefully and observe closely. These are important skills for middle school students to acquire. Think drops rather than test tubes or cups full. With solids, think in granules and pea-sized proportions.

Oldies but not Goodies

Many of the chemistry demonstrations and materials found in old science methods books are now known to be hazardous. Refer to Appendix A, p. 165, for a list of chemicals that do not belong in a middle school program and their related uses. Review all your old favorites to see if other items should be abandoned as well.

Many excellent microscale chemistry activities have been developed for the middle school level. Observing a phenomenon on a smaller scale requires students to pay closer attention to small changes and focus on detail. Students will soon discover the excitement of seeing a hypothesis confirmed, rather than seeing an experiment self-destruct.

6

Corral Your Stock

The stock supply of any chemical, even those you think are harmless, should always remain in a locked cabinet or storeroom. This is especially important with hazardous items such as corrosives, reactives, flammables, and toxics. Before class, measure out the quantities you will need and make sure all samples are labeled. Clean plastic trays or storage tubs are handy for transporting these supplies. Do not allow students in storerooms or teacher preparation areas.

No Wiggle Room

Even in their seats, middle school students seem to move all the time. You need to explain why sudden or extraneous motion can be especially dangerous during chemistry activities. But do not expect that, just because you say so, students will stop wiggling. You need to build in strategies to prevent accidents from careless movement.

For instance, have students write down what they are going to do—including precautions—rather than beginning a science activity immediately after they return from recess. Make sure everyone is seated and listening before distributing supplies and equipment. Have only one student from each group get the supplies from any single location. During chemical lab activities, have students stand. Laps make big targets for spills. Prepare a flow chart of the lab using key words, symbols, and illustrations. Show students how to avoid spills and prevent contamination of the chemicals you provide. Review procedures for students who might have been absent for the first presentation of safety precautions.

Tools of the Trade

In keeping with the idea that simpler and smaller is better, look over your inventory of science equipment. Some of what you own may be more hazardous and less useful than their newer counterparts.

Mercury-Filled Instruments: If you still have barometers, thermometers, or other measuring instruments made with mercury (the column is silver in color), you need to arrange for safe disposal immediately. The hazard posed by spilled mercury from broken instruments is serious and unacceptable. These instruments all have electronic counterparts that are no longer prohibitively expensive.

Alcohol-Filled Thermometers: Though teachers may be familiar with the classic glass thermometers for measuring temperature, many of your students have never seen one. Most students are more familiar with the electronic probes or microdot strips used by their pediatricians or the liquid crystal strips that change color at different temperatures. If alcohol-based (red line) thermometers are used, try to get those with metal safety backs. Probes that can send data directly to a computer or graphing calculator are safer and can be purchased relatively inexpensively.

Instruments for Measuring Mass: Middle school students are moving from concrete thinking to formal logic, so they need to use both manual and electronic instruments. Keep a few double-pan or triple-beam balances to help students learn and understand the concept of mass. But once the idea is well established, you will find that using electronic balances reduces the time required to take measurements and can produce more precise data. Lock up your balances when you are not using them. If you plan to leave them on counters or desktops when a room is not supervised, bolt or chain them to the work surface. Because of their value in illicit drug activity, balances are among the most commonly stolen items from science facilities.

General-Use Containers and Instruments to Measure Volume (Beakers and Graduates): Plastic containers and volume measures work well in most middle school experiments. Depending on the degree of precision and accuracy required, you

6

can often substitute simple and inexpensive paper and plastic containers available from the grocery or drug store—disposable drink cups and plates, household measuring cups, medicine cups, and calibrated droppers—for more expensive laboratory glassware. By doing this, you reduce expense and the hazard of broken glass.

You may want to teach the use of standard labware such as beakers and graduated cylinders. These containers are available in a variety of plastics that can be matched with your use and budget. Clear plastic polycarbonate containers are quite rugged and heat resistant but are also the most expensive. Polypropylene containers are translucent, making it difficult to see the liquid, and may crack more easily but are generally less expensive. Check for descriptions and suggested uses for the different types of plastics in plasticware supply catalogs. Some of the plastics are heat resistant and will not melt or deform even with boiling water but none are flameproof, so you cannot use them with burners or stovetops. If you must have glassware, be sure you order borosilicate glass that is heat resistant and flameproof. As a rule of thumb, if you are using glassware, make sure everyone is also wearing splash-proof safety goggles. When students cut or work with materials that can shatter, the goggles should be impact resistant in accordance with the ANSI Z87.1 standard. You can buy eye protection that is both splash-proof and impact

Linear Measure: Wooden meter sticks are tempting medieval weapons for some students. They can splinter. Buy flexible plastic when possible.

Sharp Instruments: Cutting tools such as razor blades and scalpels are generally too dangerous for middle school use. If you do choose to have students cut, give them blades with safety shields and teach proper technique first. Keep them secure. Have adults prepare materials ahead of time to reduce to a minimum the amount of cutting students perform. You must have disposal containers for sharps to protect personnel who handle the trash.

Tubing and Connectors: Substitute plastic tubing for glass tubing whenever possible. If you use glass tubing, make sure it is all fire polished.

Students should not cut, bend, or fire-polish glass or insert glass tubing into corks or stoppers. Even you, as an adult, should not attempt these activities unless you have had specific training to do so. Exercise extreme care and caution if you engage in this work. Cutting and inserting glass involve serious risks from breaking glass and causing permanent injury to hands and eyes. Bending or fire polishing glass adds the danger of serious burns, especially when hot glass does not look hot.

Use heat-resistant mats when you set down hot glass, and always protect your hands with something like a thick towel if you insert glass tubing. There is an apparatus available to assist with glass tube insertion, but use it with careful attention.

Heat Sources: At the middle school level, we strongly recommend that materials that need heating be prepared ahead of time by the teacher. If you are doing an activity that calls for students to observe materials while they are being heated, consider using laboratory-rated hot plates—not simple camp or home use hot plates—rather than open flame.

Some middle school classrooms have gas for use with Bunsen burners, but we do not recommend their use. If you use gas burners, you must give careful and thorough fire-safety instruction to everyone before each use.

Do not use alcohol burners. (See Chapter 3, p. 30, "Heat Without Fire," for additional explanation.)

Geared Up for Safety

Instilling a healthy respect for chemical reactions is an important goal of middle school chemistry education. When you insist that students dress appropriately for lab activities, you reinforce the significance of the laboratory work and encourage them to act like science professionals.

Safety Eyewear: Almost every chemistry experiment requires safety eyewear. In addition to the potential for chemicals entering the eyes, you must protect against the possibility of projectiles resulting from a dropped or shattered container and materials sent flying by an unanticipated release of pressure. If something can splash or splatter, put on eye protection—this includes you and any other adults in the room—and leave them on until everyone is done. Remember the eyewear should be splash-proof for chemicals and impact resistant to protect from possible projectiles. Some eyewear meets both requirements. Contact lenses need special consideration under any circumstance that requires safety eyewear. (See Chapter 10, p. 136, "Eyewear," for further explanation.)

You need to provide one pair of goggles for every person in the room. The models you select should be marked ANSI Z87.1, a voluntary standard of the safety industry and required by the U.S. Occupational Safety and Health Administration. They are

6

available in striking fluorescent colors. Regular eyeglasses or plastic shields, also called "plant visitor specs," are not acceptable substitutes for eye protection.

Splash-proof goggles don't protect against fumes. Teachers should make every attempt to avoid fumes in the classroom by making good choices in labs and making sure there is good ventilation.

Safety eyewear must be sanitized between uses. This can be done by hanging the goggles in a sanitizer equipped with ultraviolet lights. But if the eyewear must be reused immediately by the next class, there may not be enough time for disinfecting them. A simpler procedure is for departing students to drop their goggles into a sink filled with antibacterial dishwashing solution. Entering students can thoroughly rinse and dry the goggles and wear them immediately afterward. If you use this method, make sure straps are plastic rather than cloth and have plenty of soft clean towels available. Rough paper towels can scratch the plastic lenses.

Some school PTAs have raised funds to buy a pair of safety goggles for each incoming student.

Face Shields: If an experiment requires a face shield, it probably shouldn't be done in the middle school.

Aprons: A waterproof lab apron should be used whenever there is a possibility of spills, splashes, or flame. When in use, the apron ties should be securely fastened. Worn correctly, the apron can also be used to hold back loose-fitting clothing that poses hazards from knocking something over or catching on fire. Loose-fitting sleeves should be rolled up, fastened with rubber bands, or both. In general, it is better for students to stand while doing chemistry experiments to avoid the possibility of spills onto laps. Get chairs and stools out of the way so students have room to step back or make a quick exit.

Gloves: Use heat-resistant gloves or mitts for handling hot labware. Have nonlatex gloves available for cleaning spills and stains and handling preserved specimens.

Tongs: Tongs are important tools for adult use in handling hot labware, but middle schoolers are not adept at managing them and spills often occur. Avoid having students use tongs by preparing materials ahead of time or, in heating experiments, heat materials gently, let them cool before handling, and use heat-resistant gloves if necessary.

Distance Learning: Consider purchasing a demonstration video flex camera or a digital video

Hot Stuff

Here are some combinations of reasonably safe materials that can be used to demonstrate exothermic reactions. Before trying them with students, test them yourself to determine the amounts to be used.

▶ baking soda in vinegar
▶ ice-melt salt in water
▶ effervescent antacid tablet or powder in water
▶ powdered bathroom cleanser such as Ajax in water

6

camera. Digital video cameras will be replacing analog video cameras just as digital phones are fast replacing analog. It can be used to record some activity that may be too small or too dangerous for students to observe closely. Instant replay of an experiment can be valuable. A video may also be used effectively to update students who are absent for the original activity.

Things That Go Boom

Risking student safety with explosive demonstrations has never been a good idea. In the twenty-first century, with plenty of safe alternatives, it is simply not acceptable. To give students the opportunity to directly observe a chemical system that they can analyze by themselves, forgo the urge to produce a bang. Instead use special-effects photography: You can't possibly compete with it technological wonders.

You can show students the release of energy with small, controlled chemical reactions. Use a temperature probe so students can observe the results of an exothermic reaction on a small scale. Then explore ideas; if a little of this chemical reaction causes a little heat, what might a lot do? Why is it dangerous to mix unknown chemicals? An explosion, eruption, or spillover is the result of the sudden and rapid release of a lot of heat or pressure.

Do not keep in your storeroom ingredients such as ammonium nitrate that can be used to make explosives, and let students know you do not have such materials.

WHAT IF . . .

Inevitable questions that emerge from chemistry activities are "What happens when you mix . . .? Will it explode?"

Your reply should make clear to students that it is never acceptable to mix chemicals together randomly. The excitement of science is in planning and prediction. Experiments are the culmination of a careful thought process that predicts results based on extensive preparation and review of prior data and known characteristics of materials. Let students know that you find controlled observations far more fascinating. And, as Louis Pasteur said, "Chance favors the prepared mind."

Dangerous Living Through Chemistry

The toxic effect of a chemical is a relative rather than an absolute characteristic. Commonly available household chemicals can be lethal to humans, pets, plants, and the environment depending on the use to which they are put, the concentration of the

Sample Toxicity Levels of Common Chemicals

Chemical	Animal LD50*	150 lb Adult	Effect
Mercuric chloride	5 mg/kg[2]	‹7 drops	extremely toxic
Potassium cyanide	50 mg/kg	‹1 tsp	highly toxic
Formaldehyde	500 mg/kg	‹1 ounce	moderately toxic
Aspirin	5 g/kg	›1 ounce	slightly toxic
Table salt	3 g/kg	›1 ounce	mildly toxic
Glycerin	›5 g/kg	›1 pint	nontoxic

[1]Lethal dose 50 (LD50) is the dose that results in the death of 50% of test animals

[2]Dose in milligrams per kilogram of the animal's body mass

Source: Toxicities adapted from Flinn Scientific Catalog (1999).

material, and the means of exposure. Many everyday household chemicals such as rubbing alcohol, bleach, detergents, and other cleaning agents can be toxic and dangerous when mishandled. Middle school is an excellent level for students to learn about chemical safety and the hazards of misusing chemicals.

Don't use chemicals in higher concentration than necessary for any given lesson. Remember also that exposure by absorption through the mucous membranes may be far greater than by touching. And chronic exposure is a greater danger for you than for your students.

Although adolescents are notoriously suspicious of advice from adults, you have the credibility to arm your students with data and evidence rather than just an adult opinion. You can use class chemistry activities to give students first-hand evidence of hazards they may otherwise ignore or be blissfully uninformed about. Activities that combine chemistry and biology provide excellent opportunities to discuss real-world consequences of incorrectly using and handling chemicals.

Unfortunately, the natural curiosity of many middle school students leads them to explore chemicals—particularly solvents—as mood-altering drugs. Sometimes the abused substance is a legally prescribed drug. For example, a growing drug abuse problem at the middle school level involves illegal sharing of legally prescribed Ritalin. Other prescribed drugs may

Poison Control

American Association of Poison Control Centers, National Hot Line: 800 222-1222

6

be abused in a mistaken effort to enhance athletic ability. Science teachers can work with health teachers to demonstrate the negative consequences of mishandling chemicals without resorting to preaching or lecturing.

Even though you have been thorough in explaining the dangers of misusing chemicals, some students may be tempted to abuse the materials you provide for them. So carefully secure and monitor all the chemical supplies you store and distribute. Plan your lessons carefully so that explorations of chemicals are guided by rules and procedures that direct students toward safe exploration and away from random mixing and experimentation. Time your activities so there is little spare time for unauthorized explorations.

The (Not So) Sweet Smell of Success

Remember the old saying, "If it moves, it's biology, if it smells, its chemistry"? It's probably inevitable that some of your chemistry activities generate unpleasant odors. Remember that odors are a signal that chemicals are in the air. Some chemicals have short- or long-term toxic effects while others can provoke asthma or allergies. Be sure you fully understand the nature and toxicity of the chemical that is causing the odor, and do not generate fumes at concentrations that are toxic. Even when fumes have low toxicity, minimize odors by using small quantities.

In closed or crowded conditions, even slight odors can become major problems, because odors tend to excite students and may cause them to be less cautious. If the building you are in was constructed as an elementary school or the room was converted from a regular classroom, it is probably not as well ventilated as a properly constructed science room. A properly ventilated chemistry lab has fans or HVAC systems that can exchange the entire volume of room air a minimum of eight times each hour. If your room does not meet this standard, you need to make sure strong odors and fumes are not generated. Plan labs, such as decomposition experiments, that generate odor for days when the windows can be opened, and prepare students by teaching them in advance the proper way to test for an odor. Odors and fumes are another reason for choosing microscale chemistry activities.

Sample Chemical Inventory

▶ Acetic acid (white vinegar)
▶ Ammonium hydroxide (≤1 M ammonia)*
▶ Calcium carbonate (chalk)
▶ Calcium carbonate (limestone chips)
▶ Calcium hydroxide*
▶ Chlorine bleach (≥1%)
▶ Copper sulfate

(cont. next page)

The Art of Faculty Cooperation

Here's a test question: Where are the most dangerous chemicals in most middle schools? No, not in the science room or even the custodial closet. In many schools, the correct answer is the art room. Although there has been an intense effort to urge science teachers to update curricula and rid their storerooms of unsafe chemicals, art teachers have not had as much support. Many older glazes have high concentrations of toxic heavy metals that can be released during application or in a kiln. Jewelry-making classes use strong acids, but few schools have the suitable cabinets for storing those materials.

The science teacher may be asked to partner with the art department to provide security, storage, and advice. A few guidelines:

▶ Accept only chemicals with valid dates and MSDS information.

▶ Keep all stock bottles locked in suitable cabinets.

▶ Transport chemicals to or from the art room when students are not in the halls.

Attitude Is Everything

Learning by doing has a powerful place in the study of science, but students must understand in unequivocal terms they must never mix chemicals together unless a knowledgeable adult is present and explicitly gives them permission to make the specific mixture.

With care and attention, chemistry labs can be scientific and fascinating. But middle school students' natural tendency to ignore risks and forge ahead with intemperate enthusiasm cannot be cured by a single lesson or even several. Plan lessons carefully, and try each one in advance. Don't expect great skill or maturity from students the first time they do a chemistry activity. That will develop if you plan your lessons to give progressively greater responsibility to your students during the course of the year.

Sample Chemical Inventory (cont.)

▶ Denatured ethanol
▶ Glucose (simple sugar)
▶ Glucose test strips (for sugar)
▶ Hydrochloric acid ($\leq$1M)*
▶ Iron filings
▶ Isopropanol (rubbing alcohol)
▶ Magnesium hydroxide (milk of magnesia)
▶ Magnesium sulfate (Epsom salts)
▶ Methylene blue stain
▶ pH (hydrion) paper
▶ Potassium chloride
▶ Potassium iodide
▶ Potter's clay
▶ Sodium bicarbonate (baking soda)
▶ Sodium chloride (rock, kosher, and reagent forms of salt)
▶ Sodium hydrogen carbonate (antacid tablets)
▶ Sodium hydroxide (LM)*
▶ Starch (powdered)
▶ Sucrose (table sugar)
▶ Sulfuric acid ($\leq$ 1 M)*
▶ Yeast (dry)

*These items must be stored in secure chemical resistant cabinets, one for acids and one for bases.
You should not accept donated, surplus, or discarded chemicals.

6

Dear High School Colleagues (or Parent):

Thanks for the thought. But we can't accept your leftover chemicals. Our needs are different, and we can't store or use your chemicals safely.

Sincerely,

Your Middle School Partner

A LESSON IN MATERIALS SAFETY

In this lesson students become active scientists as they search for and identify potentially dangerous chemicals in their schools and homes.

Activities:

▶ Introduce acids and bases with a special "breakfast" lesson in the cafeteria. Ask students to taste a variety of drinks such as juices, vinegary salad dressing, tonic water, and coffee. Then provide cups of dark Pekoe tea and/or red cabbage juice as indicators. Each student can add ten drops of one liquid to the indicator. Classify samples as "sour" or "bitter" (acid or base) by color and effect on indicator.

▶ To explore stronger, more hazardous chemicals, ask students to put on their eye protection and nonlatex gloves. Test bleach and aspirin with the tea or red cabbage indicator and then with pH paper. Group household chemicals as strong acids and bases.

▶ Look at the labels of common household products and discuss the precautions that should be taken with each one. Have students note that strong bases can be just as dangerous as strong acids. Discuss ways of keeping the chemicals secure at home.

▶ For a final project, ask students to work with their parents to create an inventory of all the cleaning supplies in their homes. Then as a thank-you gift, each student can make a refrigerator magnet with the numbers of the fire department and poison control center for their homes. Glue laminated tag board onto small circle or bar magnets.

6

THE SAVVY SCIENCE TEACHER

Ms. G's students spend a lot of time watching water—and it's never boring.

▶ They try dissolving different substances in plain water and determine that the amount of sugar that can dissolve in water is quite different than the amount of salt that can dissolve in the same amount of water.

▶ They measure specific volumes of water and observe that the volume and density of water change as it is cooled from room temperature and finally freezes.

▶ They determine that solutions of salt in water can also change the temperature at which the water freezes.

▶ After careful instruction, they use temperature probes in water and observe the temperature changes as the water is heated to boiling.

▶ They use probes to measure the boiling temperatures of water solutions containing salt.

By midyear, students have notebooks filled with data and graphs. They are ready to explain everything from how to melt ice on a walkway in winter to how to cook pasta more quickly. By spring, Ms. G presents students with an environmental mystery: Why has most of the lawn in the front of the school grown back after the icy winter, but not on both sides of the sidewalk?

6

Connections

Good sources for MSDS information:

▶ Vermont Safety Information Resources, Inc. *hazard.com*

▶ Fisher Scientific. *www.fishersci.com*

▶ Cornell University. *msds.pdc.cornell.edu/ msdssrch.asp*

Striking Gold

Adventures with Earth and Space Sciences

Earth and space sciences—the final frontiers. Students need to climb conceptual mountains to exploit the richness and excitement of this segment of the curriculum. But, as astronauts, oceanographers, geologists, and others know, these frontiers have their inherent dangers for which explorers must be prepared. From wearing protective clothing and equipment to exercising caution and using proper techniques with tools, there is much to be taught and much to learn. Above all, remember, there's gold in down-to-earth common sense.

Earth-Shaking Science

The Earth and space sciences provide great opportunities for engaging students in real-world experiences. Most middle school students, experiencing a growing awareness of the world around them, have just the right combination of curiosity and emerging logical constructs for you to show them broader applications of the ideas they explore in your classroom. Geology, oceanography, and astronomy are disciplines that naturally support inquiry in and out of the classroom. You can find opportunities for hands-on experience around the schoolyard, in playground ruts, at highway road cuts, along shores, in and around lakes and rivers, at the oceans, and under the skies. Earth and space science topics are ideal for showing students that science is everywhere around.

But middle school students are not only curious; they also are adventuresome. Their energy often leads them to act first and think later, especially in field experiences. You'll need careful thought and planning to ensure that these exciting activities are done safely. Done properly, your students will be able to share their newfound skills and caution when exploring with family and friends at home and on vacation. Providing your students with the safest methods will bring them a lifetime of reflective observations.

7

An Earth and Space Science Room
Is Anywhere You Find It

When there are fewer science rooms than teachers, it is often Earth science teachers who find themselves moving from one science room to another, filling in during others' free periods, or worse yet, trying to teach in a regular classroom rather than a lab classroom. Perhaps this is because the Earth science curriculum seems less complicated than some of the other sciences. If you teach a nonlayered curriculum and are responsible for all the sciences, you may find that when you get to Earth and space science topics, you have less access to laboratory facilities than someone working on chemistry-associated units. If this is the case, consider it merely a challenge to adapt available facilities and a spur to take students out in the field.

Here are a few features you should try to incorporate in whatever facility you are assigned:

▶ *Furniture, such as worktables and storage shelves, that is strong and stable enough to support the weight of heavy specimens and equipment*—If possible, trade your existing furniture for something more suitable. You may find that older furniture, oak tables and workbenches from art and industrial arts classrooms, for example, may work better than newer lightweight models.

▶ *Water access, preferably hot and cold running water from sinks within the classroom*— If plumbing is not built into your room, try for a room that is close to a water source such as a custodial closet or student washroom, and then order sturdy pails and wash tubs.

▶ *Safety eye protection for everyone and a means to disinfect safety eyewear between classes*—At the end of class students can drop safety eyewear in a sink or buckets filled with antibacterial soapy water. Entering students can rinse and dry the eyewear before they use it. Be sure to have plenty of soft clean towels available and make sure the headbands are plastic and not cloth elastic.

▶ *Secure storage space for chemicals and equipment*—If you must move your program and supplies around on a cart, get one that has lockable storage space and locking wheels.

▶ *Sufficient space for students to work without bumping one another*—Your middle schoolers likely will grow and need even more room by the end of the year than they did at the beginning.

Rock and Roll

Although the National Standards now place more emphasis on cycles and systems, most middle school students will still find their first hands-on experience in Earth science beneath their feet. Soils, rocks, and minerals are the most common accessible raw materials of inquiry. In the middle school lab, rock and mineral samples present some hazards and storage challenges—and they occasionally tempt rowdy students. But they are also an ideal way to begin lessons on attributes, classification, and scientific record keeping.

No Tasting

Although some geology books or field guides still may suggest it, rocks should never be tasted for the purpose of identification.

Because rocks are so familiar, your first challenge is to teach students to respect them as scientific materials. They are heavy and potentially dangerous. Give students organizational responsibility such as keeping the heaviest samples on low shelves and making sure boxes and bins are not top-heavy or easily tipped. Although most rock specimens can be stored indefinitely on secure shelving, beware of some specimens that oxidize such as iron ores. The stains can damage nearby surfaces and materials.

Students can also help classify rocks and minerals and record precautions. Some minerals, such as heavy-metal ores, may release salts that are potentially dangerous.

Many ores and elements are toxic (e.g., uranium, cobalt), combustible at room temperature (e.g., phosphorus), or unstable (e.g., sodium, potassium) and should not be used or stored in a middle school classroom. Talc specimens may contain asbestos.

Managing Equipment

Typical Earth science equipment is usually simple, but must be strong and sturdy. As with other science materials, storage must be lockable and secure. But because Earth science equipment tends to be larger and heavier than items for other sciences, storage usually needs to be somewhat roomier and stronger. Because much of the equipment for the earth sciences is used for cutting or fracturing specimens or obtaining samples under potentially hazardous conditions, you must give students explicit instructions about appropriate as well as safe use. As a general rule, safety eyewear is needed for most Earth science activities.

Cutters, Streak Plates, and Other Sharps: Changing standards have greatly diminished the prevalence of rock and mineral identification activities in middle school earth and space science. For those of you who do use cutting implements or other sharps, make sure they are age-appropriate, that you provide a specific safety lesson on their use, and that your students fully comprehend proper use and disposal. Select items with safety shields and sheaths and make sure blades and cutting edges are covered before storing them in locked storage. Always make sure everyone uses impact-resistant eye protection when using these implements. That may not be the same as the splash goggles used for chemistry. Check.

Tips for a Tight Budget

Some supplies and equipment suitable for Earth science activities may be available at lower cost from hardware and discount stores.

If you make these cost-effective investments, be sure they are strong enough for the intended use by exuberant adolescents and include safety features such as shields, sheaths, locks, electrical grounding, and kill switches.

Because they are made of porcelain, streak plates can break, resulting in extremely sharp shards. Make sure students understand that streak plates must be handled carefully and must be used on a level surface. (See Chapter 10, "Use and Disposal of Sharps," p. 133.)

Hammers, Rock Saws, and Rock Tumblers: Earth science may entail fracturing rocks. This is not the same as randomly striking or smashing the specimens. The process always requires eye protection, direct supervision, and carefully selecting the specimen. When possible, purchase specimens that show fracture and cleavage instead of doing this yourself or with students. Choose the rock hammer with care—not just any hammer but one specifically designed for the purpose. Poorly made or improper tools can break during use and cause serious injury. Emphasize to students that this is a dangerous, scientifically precise procedure and they should not try it at home or without trained adult supervision.

Rock saws are potentially dangerous and not recommended for use in middle school classrooms. For special projects, you may wish to use a rock saw yourself when you are away from students, but be sure to use impact eye and face protection that meets ANSI Z87.1 standards and make sure your equipment has electric and hand protection. Students should not be near the rock saw. Rock tumblers can be used safely in a classroom, because they work slowly and use nontoxic grit. Their chief problems are they must be run continuously for long periods and may be very noisy.

Glues and Lacquers: If you are lacquering fossils or other specimens, provide students only a very small quantity of the coating material in a well-ventilated area. Make sure you have material safety data sheets (MSDS) on every product you use. (See Chapter 4, p. 41.) Do not use cyanoacrylic, or "super," glues, because of their potential for damaging skin and eyes. Chemical splash goggles are required.

Hydrochloric and Other Acids: An acid test is standard for identifying carbonate-containing rocks. A 10% hydrochloric acid (HCl) is sufficient. Store the stock bottle in a locked acid cabinet. Place small quantities (no more than 10 mL) in dropper bottles before class. Make sure everyone—doers and observers—wears chemical splash safety goggles. Rinse all specimens thoroughly after testing. To avoid splashing, add acid to water, not water to acid when disposing of dilute acid.

Heat Sources: Alcohol burners should never be used. There is no compelling reason for students to use open flames in middle school Earth and space science.

Experiments to show changes as water is driven off from minerals should be presented as demonstrations or on video. Hot plates can be used for convection experiments, but choose those designed for school science, not ones marketed for cooking or other household uses. Be sure you have enough power for the hot plates you intend to use, and do not use extension cords or receptacle multipliers with them. To avoid accidental spills, emphasize discipline and keep quantities small. Make sure the area you choose for the activity is not crowded with furniture. The best arrangement is to have students stand when heating materials.

Field and Stream Equipment: If you do field studies, many of the supplies will be the same as for geology activities, but most items need to be selected for easy transport and minimal breakage. Label equipment for fieldwork with numbers and assign specific numbers to individual groups. Use the smallest possible quantities, pack them securely, and make sure everything is counted before leaving the field site. Choose plastic over glass whenever possible.

For water-related activities, make sure you have water safety equipment, such as life jackets, in the amounts and types required and that everyone is properly instructed on correct use. (See Chapter 9, p. 117, "Outdoor Sites," for additional information.)

Drafting Compasses, Meter Sticks, and Other Tempting Tools: When middle school students do mapping exercises, such as finding the epicenters of earthquakes, they may use sharp tools such as drafting compasses. Meter sticks and other rulers used to take linear measurements indoors and outdoors may seem like tools for practicing fencing moves. Count all such items going out and coming in, and make it very clear you will tolerate no nonsense with their use.

Telescopes, Binoculars, and Optical Instruments: These are delicate and expensive instruments and require careful selection and handling. At the middle school level, many students are just beginning to acquire the fine motor skills to make good use of precision optical instruments. Choose relatively simple models with features you will use. Rugged may be better than powerful since greater power will produce smaller fields of view and require greater patience to focus properly. Remember to clean eyepieces to avoid contagion.

The Dirt on Dirt

Although most people associate geology with rocks, the basic scientific material for that course is soil. For middle school students, that's the best part. The study of soils can serve double duty in your curriculum—you can teach lessons in health and hygiene as well as in Earth science.

Obtain your soil samples from a source you know, and make sure animal wastes or toxins have not contaminated them. One of the most common contaminants of outdoor sites is lead paint dust from nearby buildings, bridges, and other structures that have been scraped and repainted.

Most soils are laced with molds, bacteria, and other pathogens. Although the ideal soil for safety is presterilized, it doesn't work for many lessons about naturally occurring communities of organisms. Therefore you must ensure students wash their hands after they have examined the organisms in their samples. If you are testing soils in the classroom, wash the desktops too. But don't expose students to strong disinfectants that can result in chapping and skin breaks. In most cases, liquid soap will do, or try the newer hand cleaning gels made of quick-drying alcohol formulations. Wash hands again thoroughly when the lab is done. And of course, a room used for soil studies should not be used for preparing or consuming food.

Wet and Wild

Stream tables and ripple tanks provide models of erosion and waves that help students understand what they see in the field. Although they take up a lot of space, they encourage patient observation, so they are very effective in the middle school years.

Make sure your stream table or ripple tank is securely mounted so it can't tip. You'll need a bright place for students to see the action, but lights usually mean electricity. Keep your light sources high and secure. Be sure that no one can put one hand in the water and one on the light or splash water onto the hot lights causing them to explode.

If you build stream tables or other erosion models, try to make them with fine clean builder's sand and potting soil rather than soil from outdoors. Limit the lesson to a few days, and then take the sand outside to dry. Getting rid of moist samples prevents mold growth and contamination of the classroom, a problem that can last for years.

Seeing Stars

Astronomy is an ideal science for teaching the skills that established our methods of science—accurate observation, careful record keeping, and proposing new models of the universe. With a few precautions, astronomy can provide a safe and exciting curriculum.

Don't ever let your students observe the sun directly. Your first lesson might inform students that Galileo lost his eyesight because he didn't understand the danger. The lens of the human eye concentrates solar rays in the same way that a hand lens does. Just as a magnifying lens can focus enough heat energy from the Sun to burn a hole in a piece of paper, so if you look directly at the Sun, the lens of your eye can focus enough of the Sun's rays to burn a hole in your retina and cause permanent eye damage.

Sunglasses do not provide protection for looking at the Sun, and using layers of exposed photographic film is a method too unreliable to be trusted. Teach students the pinhole/reflection method of observing solar eclipses.

If you are lucky enough to have a telescope or the opportunity to take students to a telescope facility, stargazing activities will likely require a nighttime or evening field trip. Refer to Chapter 9, p. 109, for information about field trips.

But don't think of astronomy as limited to nighttime activities. Many interesting activities that track the movement of heavenly bodies can be performed during the day. Remember the Sun casts shadows that change size, shape, and placement depending on its position relative to the object casting the shadow. A small mirror, placed in a strategic position near a window will reflect a spot of sunlight in different places in your room. Just make sure you take precautions to prevent overexposure to the Sun if you carry on outdoor astronomy activities in daytime. Under certain conditions, the moon can be seen in daylight.

Topic: astronomy
Go to: *www.scilinks.org*
Code: SML95

Excellent Eclipse Observations

Before you begin, make sure students are well informed about the dangers of looking directly at the sun—even during a solar eclipse. The shadow of a solar eclipse can be observed safely through a pinhole.

Make a small hole in a piece of tag board, and provide students with a second piece of white paper. With their backs to the Sun, have students channel the image of the sun through the small hole onto the white paper. As the eclipse approaches, the shadow of the Moon will clearly be seen across the reflected image of the Sun.

7

In the Field

The study of Earth processes can begin in the schoolyard. Observing the playground, the school building, and the sidewalks will reveal examples of erosion and weathering.

A school grounds field trip requires the same rules for proper behavior in a field study as a distant one. Before you go, discuss the proper way to travel; prohibitions against running, jumping, and shoving; and the proper way to carry equipment. Some precautions for using playground equipment are included in Chapter 8, "Perpetual Motion," p. 99.

Geology and other Earth science fieldwork may require even more planning and advance work than other science field trips, but a well-planned field study can be memorable and inspire students for a lifetime. Protective gear of some type is usually required. Depending on the site, hard leather shoes with toe protection and ankle support may be needed. If you have students who don't own anything but athletic shoes, you may need to make special arrangements to borrow, rent, or otherwise obtain the correct footwear for everyone. You may also need to use hard hats. Check in advance. If your school is undergoing any construction, you may be able to borrow hard hats from the contractors.

Physical conditioning may be necessary. If so, consider working out a plan with the physical education teachers, and be sure everyone who goes has completed the required training. If you have students with disabilities, you may also need to work with the special education team and school medical staff to ensure these students can participate to the fullest extent possible.

If you are conducting activities in or near water, water safety and swimming instruction may be needed. Here, too, the physical education department may be a good partner for your activities.

See Chapter 9, p. 109, "The Great Outdoors," for more information on field trips.

Golden Opportunities

When you teach Earth and space sciences to middle school students, you help them see the world around them with a more discerning and understanding eye. Your Earth and space science lessons are an authentic way to connect school lessons with out-of-school explorations. After their lessons with you, your students may never whiz past a road cut, mountain, desert, or shoreline, view a quarry or the night sky, or explore a cave in the same way again.

But some travel and vacation adventures may also be accompanied by inherent dangers that can be mitigated by lessons learned in your classes and during your fieldwork experiences. When traveling with family and friends, your well-instructed Earth science students will know how to help everyone explore more safely in rugged outdoor environments. You don't just teach safety lessons as a set of rules but as a way of doing things in everyday life.

In years to come, your students may be shooting the rapids or flying over irrigated fields applying the knowledge you provided in your classroom and just outside the window. They'll do it safely if you model good habits. So dress yourself in a little common sense and dig in.

THE SAVVY SCIENCE TEACHER

Mr. J's students have a problem—and so does their whole community. The grass is dying in Community Park. The trails are eroding, and the trees are losing their leaves. But his seventh grade Red Team has accepted the challenge of finding out why.

In small groups, students begin by mapping out a square with 100 m sides around the park. Each group uses global positioning system (GPS) technology to mark its quadrats on a large map in the cafeteria so the entire school can follow its progress.

With the help of parent volunteers, each group takes soil samples from its quadrat. Students use Berlese funnels to find invertebrates and inoculated sealed culture plates to test for *E. coli*. Each sample is sterilized before disposal. Using their combined data, they discover a small and dying population of soil organisms.

High school partners also gathered soil samples and then tested them chemically. The answer to the dying grass? Common road salt.

But who would put so much salt in Community Park? Plotted on the map, the results of the assays show a trail leading directly to a local car wash. There, salt has sluiced off cars that have traveled icy roads treated with salt. Red Team's next science lesson will be shared with the county drain commission.

7

Falling for Science

Physical Science May Be Simpler Than You Think

When Galileo watched the cathedral's pendulum swing, no one feared it would fall on someone's head. Leonardo's model siege engines never propelled spit wads. Madame Curie never feared that someone would steal her radium. Teaching physical science should be just that simple, but middle school students are naturals in movement, velocity, and acceleration. Your challenge is to slow them down enough so they can see the world as Newton did, "on the shoulders of giants."

Getting in the Swing

Although we wish it were different, many elementary school teachers shy away from physical science and may confine hands-on science activities to planting seeds and observing them. Thus, too many students get their first exposure to quantitative physical science in the middle school. The *National Science Education Standards* (NRC 1996) recommend that students study motions, forces, and transfer of energy during the middle school years. That almost always includes an introduction to electricity and quantitative work with the laws of motion. These are ideal topics for budding scientists. They provide opportunities for observing familiar things in new ways, recording and analyzing data, making authentic connections to the real world. Exploring the physical world requires only a few basic precautions to ensure safety.

Perpetual Motion

The bell rings. Middle school classes change. Right out there in the hall you can observe that every elbow action has an equal and opposite reaction, that momentum will carry a running mass of preteen a long way, and that it's real work to lift up a load of books. In these years, science gives students a chance to get physical—and teachers need to ensure commonsense safety is also applied.

Galileo studied mechanics by dropping things, and so can middle school students. But remember that the procedures and rules must always be age-appropriate. In middle school, it may be best to assign one student to do something for the rest of the class to observe, because, where two or more are gathered together, silliness often occurs. If an object is to be dropped from a high perch, for instance, make sure the dropper can't fall and the landing area is clear.

Playground equipment can also be used to teach physical science concepts, but remember that some students may get rough and rowdy when returning to their elementary school haunts. Be certain that the equipment you use meets the new federal standards that have been developed for playground equipment and that your proposed use falls within the scope of its intended use. Make sure that student observing and recording activities are well outside the range of moving components such as swings. For example, on a swing set, the danger area may be far greater than the length of the swing.

One of the most exciting culminating activities in physics is an amusement park "lab exercise." With a lot of structure and the normal dose of caution, middle school students can gain a lot from these trips.

Managing Equipment

Physical science equipment ranges from simple tools to sophisticated electrical meters. Here are a few common materials that might be in your curriculum:

▶ *Carpentry Tools:* Hammers, saws, and other carpentry tools can be useful for constructing a variety of projects. Refer to Chapter 7, "Tips for a Tight Budget," p. 92, and Chapter 10, "Use and Disposal of Sharps," p. 133. Make sure everyone is properly instructed in the use of the tools and that everyone, including bystanders, is wearing eye protection. Middle school students should not use power tools under any circumstances. If you have a technology education program or there is a vocational technical high school in your district, see if the students will build that apparatus you need.

▶ *Pendulums:* Safely conducting these activities depends on class discipline. Begin with short strings and rounded bobs. Before each use, check, and have your students check, that the bobs are securely fastened to their strings. Encourage careful observation and good record keeping. Teach students to begin the swing by letting go of the pendulum bob rather than pushing or throwing it with uncontrolled force.

▶ *Momentum Carts (Cars):* Be aware of the placement of ramps. Make sure they do not block walking paths or send cars zooming into the hall. Be sure cars aren't left out on the floor or any other walking area.

- *Carbon Dioxide Pellets:* These can produce significant momentum. Cars using them should be on tracks and not running freely. Use eye protection.

- *Model Rockets:* Check the legality of these devices in your district. Use only approved engines and electric igniters. During construction, make sure the cardboard ring that holds the rocket engine during launch is glued in straight. Errat, dangerous flights can ensue otherwise. Students launching rockets must be supervised and must wear eye protection.

- *Batteries and Bulbs:* Although direct current (DC) may seem safe compared to alternating current (AC) from wall plugs, batteries and bulbs must still be handled carefully. You might open a battery to show students how they are constructed, but do not allow students to dismantle batteries. Depending on their type, they are made from strong acids and bases and other substances that require care and eye protection when handling. Short-circuited batteries can cause wires to heat up enough to cause burns. Even small flashlight bulbs can be broken if roughly handled. Batteries can contain hazardous wastes that can contaminate landfills and the regular waste stream. Never open the new alkaline batteries. This was all right in the old days, but not today. You can get diagrams of the insides of batteries from the websites of manufacturers.

- *Lasers:* Generally, middle school students should not use lasers.

- *Balances:* Keep them secure; they are highly valued for illicit drug activity.

As in all science rooms, the physics location needs eye protection and sterilizing facilities, fire protection, and proper storage and disposal areas.

Sights and Sounds

To the middle school mind, *sound* is blasted through headsets, *light* is best seen in *a concert strobe*, and *"the wave"* is a group activity. As you expand your students' views, take the opportunity to instill a little healthy caution.

Many teachers encourage students to make their own sound generators or musical instruments. Make sure that percussion instruments can't shatter, string instruments can't break and send parts flying, and wind instruments don't spread germs. Once middle schoolers discover that sound is science, you may also need to consider noise control.

Hearing damage caused by loud and/or constant sound is a growing problem among young people. They use headsets, boom boxes, and other sources of loud music and sound without realizing the extent of permanent damage that can be done to their hearing. Whether you are conducting specific activities on sound or using equipment for another reason, avoid devices that generate more than 85 decibels of sound. Even at that level, the ear will accommodate by temporarily "shutting down," and

students could have trouble discriminating sounds afterward.

Use similar caution with lights. Lasers should not be used in middle school. If you demonstrate a laser pointer, include a lesson on how harmful it can be if abused. "Black" or ultraviolet (UV) lights should also be used with caution and appropriate eye protection.

Use lessons on light to reinforce good vision habits. Insist upon and model the use of eye protection at all appropriate times. This should include protection from liquid splashes, projectiles, and harmful wavelengths of light. Share information on the best light for reading and close work. Help students understand the dangers of staring directly at any bright light, particularly the Sun. (See the explanation of the lens of the eye in Chapter 7, p. 94, "Seeing Stars.")

Lightbulbs themselves pose a number of hazards. Heat generated by bulbs can cause serious burns. The bulbs are usually made of glass, so a broken glass hazard is always present. Teach students to avoid handling bulbs directly, particularly halogen bulbs. Salt and oils from bare hands can cause the bulbs to shatter if they are turned on. A splash of water can cause a hot bulb to explode.

Charge Ahead

Many physical science activities require electrical devices, either alone or interfaced with computers. Teaching students to have a healthy respect for electricity is important in school and in their daily lives.

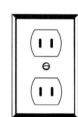

Figure 1

Classrooms in older schools are notoriously short of electrical receptacles. Don't try to solve the problem by using socket multipliers or multiple extension cords. More places to plug in does not equal more capacity. In fact, more wire produces more resistance, less usable power, and a greater fire hazard. If you trip a circuit breaker, you don't have enough capacity. Don't try it again—call maintenance.

Figure 2

All outlets should be properly grounded and all outlets near water should be protected with a ground fault interrupter (GFI). If your room does not have adequate electric service, or if the outlets do not have the proper grounding and safety features, make a request for upgrades or repairs in writing and be sure to include both the educational and safety reasons for your request. Be sure all electrical equipment you use is properly grounded and do not circumvent the ground plug with an adapter "cheater" wire.

Figure 3

If you need power in the middle of the room once or twice, make sure the cords are taped down securely the entire length with duct tape and take them back up immediately after the activity. If you need it more frequently, consider requesting a permanent outlet in the location needed.

8

Some rooms have raised floor jacks that pose a tripping hazard, others have power poles that an inattentive student may crash into, and still others have tempting pull-down plugs. The perfect system for getting power in the middle of a classroom hasn't been invented. But if you have the opportunity to renovate or re-design, recessed receptacles with lock-down caps have been rated highly by some teachers. If receptacles do not have caps, make sure there is some other way to prevent water or other liquids from getting in.

In the United States, typical household receptacles come in three types. The oldest type has two equal openings, and plugs can be inserted in any direction (fig. 1). Schools should not still have these in the walls. Newer receptacles have directional current, with one slot larger than the other (fig. 2). Televisions and some other electrical devices must be plugged in one direction, not another. The third and preferred form of receptacle has two slots of different sizes and a third opening for a ground (fig. 3). This is the only form of plug safe for a classroom.

Some devices—such as kilns, stoves, shop equipment, and theater lighting equipment—require higher voltage lines. The receptacles for these lines are generally round, with large openings arranged radially. The configuration of the socket is determined by the amperage that the circuit can safely carry so that the appliance must be exactly matched to the receptacle intended for it.

The most power-consuming devices are those that heat or cool. Very few older classrooms can support many hot plates. So what can an inquiring teacher do if there is not enough electric power? Look for low-wattage appliances. Plan activities at centers or stations so the most power-intensive work won't have to be done by everyone at the same time. Arrange to use a room with better electrical support. Do demonstrations if no other alternative is available.

Electricity follows the path of least resistance to the ground. The presence of many electrolytes makes

Form a Cadre of Electrical Safety Experts

Encourage students to become safety experts at home as well as in school. Tell them to
- make sure electric outlets are not broken and plugs fit well in them.
- never stick anything into an electrical receptacle or appliance that is plugged in—use safety covers on unused receptacles when young children are present.
- make sure lightbulb wattage does not exceed the rating of the appliance or wall socket.
- never use multiple extension cords on the same circuit or cover extension cords with floor coverings.
- if an appliance trips a breaker, turn it off until the appliance is checked.
- keep space heaters at least one meter away from walls and combustible materials.
- keep combustible materials away from halogen lamps.
- never use electrical appliances near water or electrical tools in the rain.

More tips: National Electrical Safety Foundation. *www.nesf.org/home/safety.html*

8

human tissues excellent conductors, so electric shock is an ever-present danger. Do not attempt to repair or manipulate any electrical appliance or equipment that is plugged in.

Humans are sensitive to electrical charges. Most people can sense as few as five milliamperes of direct current. As the current increases, muscles contract and spasm, and eventually the heart and diaphragm stop. Nine milliamperes from a battery or two from a wall circuit would be felt as a shock. More than 60 milliamperes from a battery or 9 milliamperes from a wall socket would cause a painful and potentially dangerous shock. Low currents can cause severe burns even if they don't threaten life.

Danger can be present even when receptacles are safe and circuits are adequate. Fuzz or lint can enter sockets. Equipment can overheat and cause fires or melt internal parts. Insulation can be nicked or damaged, causing current to flow to parts of the machine where it is not intended. Check electrical equipment and power cords carefully before each use. If something appears abraded or damaged, arcs, sizzles, heats up, flickers, or pops a circuit, don't use it.

FRAYED CORDS AND DAMAGED PLUGS

If you have directional or three-pronged plugs but the oldest—style two—equal-blade type of receptacle to put the plugs in, you may be tempted to clip off the ground, stick in an adapter with "cheater" wire, or otherwise tamper with the connection. DON'T DO IT. Damage to the appliance is the least of the problems; danger to users is a liability you should not risk. Put in a written request for electrical upgrades and do not use equipment that requires the upgraded receptacles until you have the proper electrical service.

If you find frayed or worn cords, do not patch them up with electrical tape. Likewise, do not just replace a broken plug with one of the clip-on replacements. Although the connection you make may be safe when you finish it, these types of repairs look odd to students and invite them to pick at, take apart, or otherwise undo your patch work. Instead, replace the whole cord with a molded-on three-prong plug. If you do not have the experience or skill to do so, send the device out for professional repair.

Many people consider batteries and direct current a safe alternative to wall current—and it usually is. But be cautious here, too. Don't use rechargeable batteries in series; their voltage can be unpredictable. Don't use large (9 or 12 V) batteries in classroom wiring experiments. And encourage students to be serious at all times.

A Classroom Electrical Safety Tour	Y/N
1. Are cords and plugs intact? (No frays, staples, or taped repairs.)	
2. Are receptacles carrying the proper load? (No multiplied sockets.)	
3. Is the circuit breaker panel clearly labeled and free from obstruction?	
4. Are outlets appropriate, firm, tight, and unbroken?	
5. Are appliances unplugged when not in use?	
6. Are appliances equipped with grounds?	
7. Are all the grounds being used?	
8. Are appliances far from water?	
9. Are circuits protected with ground fault interrupters?	
10. Are all cords out of the way of foot traffic and exposed rather than covered by carpets or under boxes or furniture?	

Source: Sarquis. 2000.

Although the Van de Graaff generator is a time-honored and exciting demonstration, it is also a potential hazard. Treat this voltage generator with respect.

If you teach electricity, you will eventually make electromagnets. Resist the temptation to use higher voltage on your devices. Increase the power with more turns of wire.

Some of the greatest dangers from electricity occur outdoors. Spend some time acquainting students with lightning hazards. A firm rule: If you hear thunder or see lightening, take shelter—no exceptions.

What's Inside

A popular and authentic middle school exercise has been to dissect common household items to study design technology. But technology may have become so complicated that equipment is no longer self-descriptive or transparent. So much has been built into the microscopic chip, you can look at a modern electronic device all year and have no idea how it works. Also, electrical devices have inherent hazards, including capacitors that hold charges even though the device is not plugged in and glass parts that may be under negative pressure and easily imploded even with careful handling.

If you still want to engage your students in a dissection activity, choose good old-fashioned mechanical devices like wind-up clocks and timers, old point-and-shoot or disposable cameras, manual staplers, pencil sharpeners, binoculars, or tire-changing jacks rather than electrical appliances or electronic equipment. You must still take care to avoid cuts from sharp parts and wear safety eyewear in case of loose springs or other flying parts, but the hazards are fewer. With mechanical devices, middle school students should find it easier to make the connection between form and function of the parts. However, be sure that the objects you examine are no longer needed, in case they cannot be reassembled.

The Computer Age

Computers have added a new level of challenges to classroom design. Classrooms designed and built prior to the use of computers almost never have sufficient electrical service in needed locations. Surge protectors and universal power sources (UPS) are needed to protect valuable and sensitive computer equipment from power surges and outages.

Computers and related equipment also require additional space. They should not be placed near sinks and should be spaced far enough apart so students can use them without interfering with other equipment and each other.

If your room isn't equipped with sufficient power in the appropriate locations for full desktop computers, consider laptops. The batteries that are used for computers and calculators are usually specialized for the use and the device. If they can be re-charged, follow the instructions exactly and use the supplied recharger. Do not mix these batteries with those used for science and other activities.

Expert Advice

Although there are challenges in providing a good physical science program, there are many advantages too. The safety skills you teach have outstanding value in the real world of your students. You may want to enlist expert help to review the conditions in your room or to make a presentation to your students about safety measures they regularly apply in the conduct of their work. You might call your local power company for a good safety presentation or your local building inspector for expert help in providing an improvement plan. Be sure you meet in advance with expert speakers and prepare the speakers and your students so the visit is a fruitful one.

THE SAVVY SCIENCE TEACHER

Ms. T's eighth graders think they are mature—until they return to the local elementary school to study friction on the playground slide. Then all the kid in them re-emerges. Because she knows they will get silly, she prepares for these expeditions with specific jobs for each scientist: the masser, the timer, the data recorder, the friction technician. By the time they return to the "big kid's school," Ms. T's students have concentrated on science enough to see their old playground with a new eye.

Next Ms. T has her students explore potential and kinetic energy by building model roller coasters to test theories and ideas. She keeps the students constantly busy with structured tasks, and makes sure that no one has time or opportunity to abuse the marbles, glue, and Styrofoam tubes they use.

These activities culminate with Ms. T's annual trip to the local amusement park to time real roller coasters. They form small groups with adult volunteers, and have plenty to observe, measure, and analyze before they reach the wieners and sodas. No student has a chance to act anything but scientific during Ms. T's physics lessons.

Connections

▶ McCullough, J., and R. McCullough. 2000. *The Role of Toys in Teaching Physics.* College Park, MD: American Association of Physics Teachers.
▶ Sarquis, M. 2000. *Building Student Safety Habits for the Workplace.* Middletown, OH: Terrific Science Press.

8

The Great Outdoors
Field Trips Near and Far

Mr. H's class knew Rule Number 2: Nothing could be collected at the field site. But Gini and Mai just had to have a souvenir for a sick friend. They certainly weren't interested in the scat or scraps of fur they'd observed, but there was that amazing green plant that poked right through the spring snow. Their treasure went in the backpack, and the girls felt sure that their secret was safe—until their stolen skunk cabbage warmed up on the bus. At least it wasn't poison ivy!

Classroom Limits

Your own classroom is rich with resources and activities, but some things simply can't be done there. A strong investigative science program depends on providing students with the opportunity to collect and analyze data. Some data can be collected in the classroom, but you may have to go elsewhere to collect real-life data—traveling to an exhibit, some equipment, or some experience that cannot be duplicated in your school. Well-planned field trips are a vital part of the total educational program. They play an important role in helping students relate basic concepts learned in the classroom to practical work and applications in the real world. But, in today's tight-budget, cost-cutting era, you need to take more time to ensure the few resources available to support off-campus activities are used effectively. The purpose and goals of the trip need to be integrated with the learning expectations of your program. And, just as important, the activity needs to be planned well ahead of time to ensure a safe and productive experience.

Because you will be working outside the confines of your classroom, in addition to the normal safety issues, you now need to take into account that the venue may be larger, less familiar, less structured, and generate more excitement.

9

Most middle schoolers don't go anywhere without their backpacks—security when they move into new environments. You need to make safety procedures so valuable, so meaningful and intrinsic that students will consider them a vital part of their mental backpacks, never to be left behind.

A Journey of a Thousand Miles …

Consider making your first field study one that can be done just outside your building. This way, you can test the maturity of your students and their ability to respond to your instructions in a more open environment. You can begin training helpers to assist with monitoring the students' work and safety in a less formal setting than your classroom.

Use that first field experience to set expectations and establish structure. Organize the groups in advance, and provide all the directions in the classroom before moving outdoors. Make boundary restrictions very clear, and caution students not to disturb other classes or neighbors. Be clear about how much time your students will have. Prepare them for the signal you will use—waving a signal flag, blowing a whistle, or ringing a bell—for a two-minute warning and when time is up.

Allow time for students to regroup and return to the classroom. Do not allow the trip to continue through dismissal time. Make sure there is closure in the classroom and follow up indoors before everyone leaves for the next class. Collect the assignment or product as soon as the students return and ask them to debrief the experience, including an assessment of their own behavior. Have students suggest ways to improve procedures for the next trip. If this is successful, you are ready for a longer out-of-class activity.

With each subsequent activity, increase the time and degree of independence you give students. As these activities grow longer, plan to make some significant change within the activity after about 10 to 15 minutes of work. It doesn't mean you have to return to the classroom, but, just as in regular classroom activities, you need to refocus the students by changing the pace, the activity, the groups, or just stopping for a break before continuing.

FAIR PLAY

Middle schoolers place high value on fairness and take great umbrage if they believe they or their fellow students are treated unfairly. Take advantage of this characteristic and plan to have your students participate in creating the safety rules that will govern their behavior outside the formal classroom. Before the out-of-class activity, divide students into the groups they will be working in. Ask the groups to work together in class to create a list of the problems that might occur and to suggest rules and procedures for prevention. You may be surprised at how perceptive middle school students can be and how tough they will be when creating rules for themselves.

9

Twenty-Minute Field Trips

Practice structured fieldwork and establish expectations for safe and serious conduct in informal settings with quick outdoor excursions. When you choose a simple phenomenon to observe, it is easier to find and limit the number of variables that need to be controlled in the observations (e.g., time of day, location, measuring instrument, and technique for measuring). And by beginning with a simple field activity in a nearby, familiar location, you can also more easily observe and identify possible safety hazards. Allow for time to get outside and choose a task that is meaningful and easily completed.

Here are some you might assign:

▶ Count and classify the plants around the school building.

▶ Map and plot the location of trees on campus; measure height and girth of each tree.

▶ Lay out a 1 m² quadrat and count the populations of grass and dandelions. Record and compare the size of populations.

▶ Measure student heights and lengths of shadows cast for in-class ratio calculations and comparisons with findings of other classes at different times of day.

▶ Examine a crack in the pavement and see what is living in it.

▶ Take a crayon rubbing of the bark of a tree on the school property for a later scavenger hunt.

▶ Find out the mass of sidewalk chalk required to write your name in 10 cm high letters.

Be Prepared

As part of your lesson planning you must thoroughly examine the site. If at all possible, every person who will be accompanying you and your students should also preview the site. Your checklist of things to do at the site should include surveying the site for possible safety hazards.

Scout It Out

▶ What are the natural boundaries of the site?

▶ Are there hazards within the boundaries of the site?

▶ Are there hazards accessible from the site?

▶ Is there any toxic vegetation?

▶ What is the likelihood of insect hazards (e.g., deer ticks, mosquitoes, bees, spiders)?

▶ Are animal encounters likely?

▶ What are the tripping or falling hazards?

▶ Can you see and monitor all students at all times?

▶ Are there private property/trespass issues?

▶ Is there a chance of the presence/intrusion of other groups or individuals?

▶ What are the conservation restrictions?

▶ How much sun are students likely to get?

▶ Are there water hazards?

▶ Where are the rest room and washing facilities?

▶ What is the nearest emergency medical facility?

▶ What is the nearest source of help?

▶ Where is the nearest phone?

9

If you expect to use staff or consultants from the field site, then a full and detailed planning session should include a discussion of exactly how you will prepare your students, what you expect your partner/consultants to do with your students, and enough information about your group and individual students for the "outsider" to know what to expect and how to work safely and effectively with your class.

You must determine clearly and exactly who will be in charge of each and every student during every activity and at every moment of the activity. The greatest poten-

HOW MANY IS ENOUGH?

There is no clear ratio of adults to students that can be applied to fieldwork. The right number depends on such disparate factors as the distance and location of the site, the hazards at the site, the nature of the activities you have planned, the skill and experience of the chaperones, and the behavior of the students in your class. However, here are some guidelines to help:

▶ Do not count yourself in the adult/student ratio or assign yourself to a specific group. You need to be available to monitor the overall activity and support your helpers.

▶ Do not count special education aides in the adult/student ratio. In groups with special education students, the aide(s) or co-teacher should be an addition to the subgroup chaperone.

▶ Every student in a chaperone's group should be clearly visible and reachable by the chaperone at all times.

▶ If a student has a record of being disruptive, additional adults may be required. You may make having an accompanying parent a condition of attendance.

▶ Include enough adults to allow one or more adults to go for help or stay with an injured student while still having enough adults to properly supervise the remaining students.

▶ Make sure you conform to any adult/student policies required by school authorities.

Whatever the number of adult chaperones, students should understand that they are responsible for monitoring their own behavior and each other's.

9

National Science Teachers Association

WHO'S IN CHARGE?

It is important for your students to understand that chaperones will provide support, advice, and some guidance, but are not intended to police the students. The students themselves must take that responsibility. Set up your group procedures so mutual responsibility among group members is built in. In planning activities, embed self-monitoring activities that require students to come together at frequent intervals to share and record data and make a contribution to the group before proceeding further. For example, on a paper worksheet or electronic database, require reports from every member of the group before going on to the next data collection task.

tial for problems arises when one adult assumes another adult is responsible for a child or group without being certain the other adult is in place and has explicitly recognized and accepted the responsibility.

As discussed in Chapter 1, keep in mind that you are responsible for everything that is done with your class at all times. That is key to recognizing the steps you need to take in preparing for a field trip. Even though there are extra adults, remember it is your responsibility to thoroughly prepare your assistants for their duties. Do not invite or accept any other person's assistance in your class and with your students unless you have reviewed the entire plan, purpose, and procedure for the activity.

A few quick comments five minutes before the activity begins are not enough. Remember, most parents have not supervised more than a half dozen teens at any one time. What you do every day out of habit is not necessarily second nature or inherently obvious to even the most responsible parent, student teacher, or aide. Think of the many things you have learned the hard way and make sure your volunteers do not do the same! And if you do use parents as chaperones, be sure they do not bring younger siblings or any other guests along.

Many field trips also incorporate special guests or field experts. Prepare your students—and the guest experts—before they meet. Find out if your expert has worked with middle schoolers. Though your guests may be experts in their fields, they may need your assistance in preparing to eliminate jargon and use an appropriate level of vocabulary for middle school students. They may also need your help organizing and breaking up the activities they lead so students stay on task. If your field expert has not prepared one, you might have to prepare a structured data or response sheet that students must complete during the activity. Preview the topic with your students so they are prepared to raise some good questions as they work with your guest.

9

TO GO OR NOT TO GO

What to do with the disruptive student whose behavior you do not trust in an out-of-classroom environment? There is no simple answer for this. The factors are many:

- What is the history of the behavior problem? Is it better or worse under certain conditions, and how do the conditions compare with the conditions you expect in your fieldwork?

- What is your school/district policy? Are administrators willing to provide additional personnel (perhaps themselves) to accompany this student?

- Is this a problem documented in an individual education plan (IEP) for the student? If so, what are the recommendations and special provisions?

- Have you discussed the student's behavior with the parents/guardians? Are they willing to cooperate and support your recommendations, perhaps willing to escort their child? Are the parents willing to give you the authority and resources to send the student home mid-trip if the behavior is unacceptable?

- What provisions can be in place for immediate intervention and sending the student home if things do not work out?

- What is the potential effect of this student's behavior on the rest of the students? Can you guarantee protecting everyone else if this student becomes disruptive?

Fieldwork, by its very nature, is a much more complex activity than classroom work. If anything, it requires more structure and attention to details than regular class/lab activities. Yes, it is important to recognize that you need to plan to include everyone in all activities. With careful thought and planning, almost all students, even those with behavioral disorders, can be accommodated. But it is also important to recognize there are some circumstances and students that cannot be accommodated successfully with the means available to you. That is when you need to make a critical decision—to go ahead with the field activity and provide an in-school alternative for the student(s) whose behavior cannot be accommodated or to forgo the field activity or radically modify it for everyone. A field trip gone wrong is worse than no field trip at all, for you and for your students. This is a time when being a professional means you recognize the limitations of your own and your school's resources.

9

How Are You Going to Get There?

The buddy system is a must for any off-site activity. Even if you are asking students to work in small groups, it is critical that every student be specifically paired with another student, and each one must be aware of what is happening to the other. It is too easy for even a group of three or four to get so engaged in some task or discovery that one missing member might not be noticed immediately. Make sure all students know who their buddies are, who else is in their group, and which chaperone has been assigned to their group.

Establish a specific meeting place and make the meeting place the very first stop with all your students and chaperones. Make sure that everyone knows when and under what circumstances to stop the activity and report immediately to the meeting place.

Walking may be the most convenient way of reaching an outdoor site. It gives you the greatest flexibility and the lowest cost. Be sure you review crossing and waiting rules, especially if you are anywhere near roadways, driveways, bike paths, or other hazardous crossings. You will need an adult at the beginning and at the end of the group. Put your slowest walkers at the front so they can set the pace. Take a head count before you begin, as you arrive, and at key points in between.

Public transportation—buses, trains, trams, trolleys, subways, ferries—may be available. It may be an economical option, as well as an opportunity to teach your students how to use public transportation safely and responsibly. If you use public transportation, remember that it will be more difficult to get a group on and off the vehicle during scheduled stops than if you were traveling alone. So make sure you review embarking and disembarking instructions carefully with students and chaperones. You do not want an individual or equipment left behind on a vehicle or a platform. If there is a platform manager or "host" at the station, introduce yourself and your group.

A school bus or chartered bus is the most common method of transporting students to and from field sites. To ensure you get to the correct place at the right time and return as expected, you will need to supply written plans and instructions that include:

Keeping Count

On a field trip, check the number of students and adults

▶ before leaving the classroom
▶ when beginning walking or during boarding of vehicle
▶ at least once per hour at the site
▶ prior to moving from one site to another
▶ upon arrival at each new location
▶ at every boarding of vehicle
▶ prior to departure
▶ upon return to school

9

- Number of adults, number of students
- School pick-up time
- Destination and drop-off location at the trip site
- Field site departure time
- School return time and pickup location

Make sure you take attendance after every stop, and do not allow students to change buses. Although research data are mixed with regard to the effectiveness of safety belts on school buses, the data are clear that using monitors on school buses increases safety because they minimize driver distraction. For this reason, at least one chaperone should ride with students on each bus. You may have one of the chaperones drive to the field site in a separate vehicle in order to have an additional vehicle available in case of emergency, but all buses must have at least one adult supervisor who is not the driver.

Whether you travel on foot or by public or private transportation, when you are off-site, you and your students will most likely come into contact with people you don't know. You must discuss ahead of time appropriate and inappropriate interactions with "strangers." Your students must know that courteous behavior is expected but that they need to limit their conversation and contact. They must never divulge personal information, accept any items, permit personal contact, or become separated from the group and assigned chaperone. Instruct students to immediately report to you or their designated chaperone if they experience any unwanted, unusual, or uncomfortable contact from anyone, including authority figures and persons in charge of the site you are visiting.

When you return, make sure all students are picked up before you leave the school.

Planning for Public Transportation

- Check schedules
- Contact the transportation authority to be sure they can accommodate your group with their regularly scheduled runs
- Review procedures and expectations with chaperones and students
  - Interaction with strangers
  - What to do if someone gets separated from the group
  - Where you expect to get on and off
  - Who will pay the fares
  - Courtesy and consideration

Museums, Zoos, and More

A visit to an informal science center is most effective when there is thorough advanced preparation. The most productive and the safest of such visits are those with a narrowly focused purpose that has been carefully discussed in advance with the educational staff of the institution to be visited. The facility may have worksheets or preplanned exercises that you can modify by embedding your group structure. If not, visit first and develop your own.

Preparatory classroom work before the visit is also important. The greatest potential for disappointment and trouble arises when the visits are general tours, or when the teacher simply turns students over to the institution staff. If students do not have a specific series of tasks to complete, questions to answer at the site, and objectives that are an integral part of your school program, they are easily tempted to race through the site, hide or get lost, cause disturbances, harm exhibits, and hurt themselves.

With a clear focus, students are much less likely to amuse themselves in unproductive or dangerous ways. Your presence and participation with the institution's instructors are also imperative to connect the field site experience with classroom work. You are the one who knows your students best, and you are responsible for knowing exactly what they have been taught and what they have experienced, even if you are not the lead instructor.

Outdoor Sites

Whether the site is as near as just outside the school doors or far enough away to require a bus or even an overnight stay, you need to check out the possible hidden hazards, especially if you are using an unfamiliar location. You should also make sure the site does not carry restrictions for use and access. Check this particularly with conservation land, wildlife preserves, and private property, and make sure there is no hazardous materials contamination.

We Have Met the Enemy and They Are Us

If there is a structure such as a bridge or tower near your chosen site, expect temptation. Do not count on students to read and obey "Danger, Keep Out" signs. Be clear and specific. You should also find out if there have been refurbishing projects that could have taken lead paint off the structure and allowed lead dust to contaminate the area. If utilities have right-of-ways in or near a site, identify any high voltage hazards. Sites near utilities and manufacturing and research facilities should be checked for the possibility of toxic wastes. Areas formerly used for military training may contain unspent munitions. Turn these possible hazards into a safety learning experience.

Water, Water Everywhere

One of the most common extended field trips in middle schools involves water sampling. Check your site in advance. What is the footing like near the water's edge? Is the water biologically or chemically contaminated? Will there be mosquitoes? Are there snakes, alligators, snapping turtles, or other potentially harmful organisms?

Is the water deep enough that you'll need water safety equipment and clothing, boots or other footgear, and gloves? Remember, students can drown in very little water if they are careless or unsupervised. Regulation life preservers should be on and not just available. In the worst case, who would be responsible for rescue or CPR (cardiopulmonary resuscitation)? For trips that require use of a boat, make sure the suppliers and operators of each vessel meet all licensing, safety, and insurance standards and requirements.

Water studies may use chemicals or probes. All equipment used on a field trip should be tried in the classroom first. Practice the procedures in advance. Incorporate responsibility for maintaining and operating the equipment in group tasks and procedures. If you use chemicals, you will need to bring material safety data sheet (MSDS) information along with the kits. Establish rules for where samples can be collected and how deep students can explore for them, and don't tolerate any less-than-professional behavior.

An Animal's Home Is Its Castle

In the field, your students will trespass into the habitats of animals. Teach them to respect these homes and the ecosystems they visit. Prepare by asking questions: What animals are likely to be found at or near your site? What is the normal behavior of these animals? What are signs that the animal may be sick or injured? You do not have to be the expert on this, but you do need to check with a naturalist or guide who is familiar with the location and can advise you thoroughly and accurately.

As a rule, students should not approach any animal—living or dead. The normal behavior of animals is to hide or run from humans. One that approaches your group or does not scurry away is more likely to be sick or injured and should be left alone. Teach students to avoid nests or dens. An animal protecting its young is likely to be very aggressive. Above all, do not touch or approach a sick or injured animal—do not attempt a rescue or try to bring it back to your classroom. This is usually illegal (see Chapter 5, "Call of the Wild," p. 65).

A camera—digital or disposable—can be a great addition to your safety supplies. Asking students to photograph organisms may help them resist the temptation to capture them. Assigning photo data collection keeps students on track and helps you keep track, too.

You need to be aware of insects that are indigenous to the area and whether they could carry infectious human disease (e.g., Lyme disease, West Nile virus, dengue fever, encephalitis). Check with your district medical services if you have any questions or doubts.

To ensure that allergies and personal preferences are dealt with, ask parents/guardians to supply insect repellents for students if needed. Students need to understand the repellents they use may affect others, so use sparingly. Check with the district medical authority as to the potential toxicity of repellents that contain DEET. Determine whether anyone on the trip has allergies to bee stings or other insect bites and what you are required to do about it. See Chapter 10, "First Aid," p. 132, for information about using EpiPens to forestall an anaphylactic reaction.

Parsley, Sage, Rosemary, and Thyme

Vegetation in an outdoor area can also pose hazards. To begin with, nothing should be tasted or eaten. An exception may be allowed if you are working with a facility formally developed for outdoor education and with specific "wild" specimens deliberately cultivated or identified for a tasting activity. But do not permit students to taste anything not specifically cultivated for eating.

Pollen and spores may cause allergic responses. Be sure to check for allergic sensitivities among your students and assistants. If you have sensitive students, you may want to avoid outdoor activities altogether when pollen counts are high.

Plants can also cause serious irritation on contact. The best known are members of the *Rhus* family, commonly called poison ivy, poison oak, poison sumac, and poison elder. These plants are widespread in outdoor areas and may have different appearances in different habitats and seasons. Learn how to identify them and teach your chaperones and students to do the same. (See the illustration in Chapter 5, p. 62.) If you expect to encounter *Rhus* species on your trip, carry products that can be applied immediately if skin contact is made with the plants.

Some people mistakenly believe they are immune to the irritants in these plants because they have come into contact with poison ivy or its relatives without developing the classic itching and blistering response. In fact, sensitivity to the antigens can develop as a result of a series of exposures, with each subsequent contact resulting in stronger response.

The saps of many plants are serious irritants, particularly milky-looking saps. Students should be taught to avoid touching plants they are unfamiliar with and to wash thoroughly following accidental contact. Be sure to warn against rubbing of eyes that may transfer substances from the hands to the eyes.

Campfires have sometimes been included in overnight trips. However, current practice is to avoid such an activity. The safety issues include accidentally starting an uncontrolled fire and the production of highly toxic fumes if the wrong wood or twigs—e.g., oleander or *Rhus*—are included.

Make sure student wash their hands before eating and preparing food. Carry alcohol gel hand cleaner with you.

The Sun Also Rises

We now know there is reason for serious concern about skin damage caused by exposure to the Sun. Excessive exposure when young greatly increases the risk of skin cancers many years later. That means hats, long-sleeved clothing, and sunblock are necessary precautions for everyone working outdoors. Be sure lips and ears are also protected. Heat and dehydration also must be considered. Make sure the work area does not get too hot—or too cold—and that that everyone remembers to drink plenty of fluids.

LIGHTNING STRIKES

Lightning is a form of electricity with extremely high voltage, produced by charges in the upper atmosphere. Lightning strikes somewhere on Earth 100 times each second, and each year about 1,000 people are killed by it. Many more are hurt.

Because lightning follows the best conductor to reach the ground, it is more likely to hit a standing human being than the flat ground around the person. If you can see lightning or hear thunder you are at risk: Seek shelter in a large building or an enclosed vehicle. Never stand under a tree or near a tall, projecting structure that might provide a conducting path for the lightning bolt to reach the ground.

9 What's the Weather?

You may not be able to control the weather, but you better make sure you're prepared for it. Know what the variations in temperature and weather can be at the site you choose. What are the risks of sudden storms or flooding? Make sure you know, and make sure you have a shelter and evacuation plan.

Once you have obtained the information you need to fully understand the site and its potential hazards, you need to plan training for your chaperones and lessons for your students. These lessons should alert students to the hazards and give explicit instructions on how to avoid problems. They should begin before the trip and then be reviewed and enhanced at the site as closely as possible to when and where the hazard is likely to arise.

Equipment and Supplies

When planning for an outdoor activity, you need to think about two categories of equipment and supplies:

▶ Items needed to complete the planned activities

▶ Items needed to promote group safety

You also need to make sure equipment used outdoors is sturdier and less breakable than what you might use in the more controlled environment of your classroom. Try to avoid anything made of glass and anything fragile or brittle—for instance, use plastic sampling containers rather than glass, metal probes rather than glass, plastic hand lenses and water magnifiers rather than regular microscopes.

Weight and bulk should also be considered. Make student pairs or groups responsible for carrying and accounting for specific items, and then make sure that the materials are packed for safe transport and are light enough for the students to handle easily. Plan sufficient time for equipment to be returned, counted, and repacked before leaving the field site.

What's Not Needed

Certain items do not belong on field trips—or in student packs on field trips:

▶ axes, knives, and similar hardware

▶ radios and compact disc players—headsets and video games may help on long bus rides, but make sure that sound is turned down to avoid distracting the driver

▶ wrapping and packaging that might be discarded at the field site—use recyclable packing materials whenever possible; plan to carry out any trash that you may create at the site

Dress and footwear should not be left to chance or imagination. Make sure you provide students and parents a list of clothing and shoes needed for the outdoor adventure. Dressing in layers is a useful strategy, allowing for adjustments to be made at the site. Hats are a good idea on both hot and cold days. In sunny weather, they provide shade; in cold weather, they protect from loss of body heat. Shoes should provide good support for the arches and ankles and have nonslip soles. Open-toed shoes, sandals, thongs, and slipper-style shoes are inadequate for fieldwork. Extra toe protection and waterproofing are pluses.

Communicate dress requirements clearly to parents and offer help if their students don't have the items. Many students don't own the correct shoes or hats; others may not have support at home to make sure they are ready. Your school or class parent group may be able to assist students who have financial or other difficulty in obtaining dress and footwear for fieldwork. Be equally clear about items that should not be brought along, especially heavy and unwieldy items and items that could distract students from educational tasks and safety precautions.

9

What to include in your first aid kit depends upon the hazards of the site. Plan your first aid kit item by item rather than generically. Bring any emergency medical information and permissions along. Make sure that you have sufficient drinking water or other beverages for the duration of the trip. As a consequence, you also need to plan for the availability of rest rooms.

Be sure to bring trash bags to clean up your work areas and haul out trash.

If your field trip might take you into isolated areas, bring whistles, mirrors, emergency lights, and other equipment to signal for help.

Overnights

By middle school, students are often ready for an overnight field trip. Some are conducted at the beginning of the year as part of team-building activities, others occur midyear as special events in the middle school year, still others are culminating activities. In any case, extensive inclusion of activities embedded in the curriculum, or activities that cross disciplines focuses student attention and may also reduce anxiety and homesickness for students who may never have been away from home overnight. While the extensive precautions necessary for overnight trips would be beyond the scope of this book, many of the tips in this chapter apply.

Choose your destination and activities with the developmental level of your students in mind. The exciting cave explorations and white-water trips you enjoyed as a high school or college student are not appropriate for middle schoolers. Even the city trips that were acceptable five years ago may require greater caution than in the past. Think about your class, your community, and your budget. Make memories, not headlines.

9

Plan for students to help research and prepare their educational tasks on the trip, and prepare the chaperones thoroughly ahead of time. That will make the overt purpose of the trip more meaningful, and leave you time to prepare the safety precautions. Bring along the students' emergency contact and medical release information. Establish a phone chain for notifying parents/guardians of changes in plan, emergencies, and to confirm pickup times.

Middle school students differ greatly in their travel experiences. Don't overestimate what they know. They may have no experience with mass transit, hotel procedures, or sanitary precautions. Some students have only eaten out at fast food restaurants. They'll need very specific directions for packing. Enforce strict boundaries in the hotel and/or camping facility, both physical and regarding whom they contact. Set a curfew and make sure it sticks. Even with a curfew, students may not get a full night's rest. Don't expect to sleep much yourself!

Be sure you have a clear plan for sending a student home mid-trip in case of injury, emergency, or unacceptable behavior. Have emergency plans in place should you or a chaperone become sick or injured. If you will be in territory without immediate help, make sure everyone—students and adults—knows where and how to call for outside assistance. For some students with disabilities or special medical needs, you may need a qualified medical professional accompanying your trip.

Permissions

Your district or school may have a standard form permission slip. If so, you should begin with that document. However, because science field trips may entail more complexity than other field trips, make sure you include additional information that alerts parents to the nature of the activities planned and the special preparations that might have to be made (e.g., clothing requirements). Request, too, that parents make you aware of special needs that their children may have (e.g., allergies) even if they have already done so previously.

Your permission slip cannot relieve you or the school of liability for student safety. But it is an important legal document to show you were well organized and had planned carefully. Be sure to have the document(s) you use approved by your district's legal counsel. Sample health and medication administration forms are on the next two pages.

9

PARENTS'/GUARDIANS' HEALTH INFORMATION FORM

Source: The Brookline Public Schools, Mass.

For overnight, out-of-state, and out-of country field trips

Child's name _____ Date of Birth _____

Address _____ Telephone # _____

Parents/Guardians

Name _____ Work Phone # _____

Name _____ Work Phone # _____

Family Doctor _____ Telephone # _____

Emergency Contact Person (If parents/guardians not available)

Name _____ Phone # _____

Address _____ Work Phone # _____

HEALTH INFORMATION

1. Is there a PEANUT, BEE STING, or INSECT allergy?____If yes, treatment_____

_____

Any other allergies (food, aspirin, etc.)?____ What?_____ If yes, treatment _____

_____

2. Does your child have any medical condition?_____If yes, state diagnosis, treatment, medication _____

3. Has your child been exposed to any communicable diseases within the past 21 days? ____ If yes, specify _____

4. Is there any factor that makes it advisable for your child to follow a limited program of physical activity, i.e., heart, recent fracture or surgery, asthma, abnormal fear? _____ If yes, specify in which ways you wish his/her program limited.

_____

5. To protect your child from any possible embarrassment, does he/she wet at night?_____ sleepwalk _____?

6. Please list date of the most recent tetanus shot _____

7. Is your child bringing medication, including over-the-counter and prescription? _____ If yes, complete the Medication Administration Form on the reverse side.

*Medications MUST be properly labeled in their original containers.

9

Parents/guardians will be contacted in case of serious sickness or accident. However, in the event of an emergency situation that requires immediate medical attention I, the parent (guardian), hereby give permission to the physician selected by the director or the trip leader in charge to hospitalize, secure proper treatment for, and to order injection, anesthesia, or surgery for my child as named above.

Signed: _____ Relationship: _____ Date: _____

MEDICATION ADMINISTRATION FORM

Each medication (including vitamins and supplements) must have a separate listing and complete instructions or the medication cannot be administered.

Child's name _____

1. (Medication) _____

(Dosage/How much) _____ (Frequency/How often) _____

(Diagnosis/Symptoms/What is this being administered for?) _____

_____

2. (Medication) _____

(Dosage/How much) _____ (Frequency/How often) _____

(Diagnosis/Symptoms/What is this being administered for?) _____

_____

3. (Medication) _____

(Dosage/How much) _____ (Frequency/How often) _____

(Diagnosis/Symptoms/What is this being administered for?) _____

_____

YES	NO	
_____	_____	My child may be given Tylenol.
_____	_____	My child may be given Benadryl.
_____	_____	My child may use insect repellent.
_____	_____	My child may use sunscreen.

Prescribed medication **must** be in a prescription bottle with a pharmacy label containing the child's name, the name of the medication, the dosage, and directions for administration. All nonprescription medication must be in the **original** container with directions for use, labeled with the child's name, and with a licensed prescriber's note.

Signed: _____ Relationship: _____ Date: _____

9

Special Needs

Special needs students can and should be included in all planned field activities. Many outdoor facilities are now equipped with ramps for wheelchair access, Braille trail signs for the sight impaired, and other modifications to promote accessibility. In some cases, teachers and students helped design and prepare these accommodations.

Helium Balloons and Notes in Bottles

Classes used to prepare helium balloons and bottles with notes and return postcards. After the balloons were released outdoors and the bottles were thrown into the ocean, students eagerly awaited messages that would tell them how far the balloons and bottles had traveled.

We now know that, when the balloons disintegrate, the helium released can damage the ozone layer of the upper atmosphere and the containers cast into the sea harm sea creatures that might swallow them or otherwise come in contact with them. We strongly recommend you refrain from helium balloon and bottle note activities.

Bring emergency medical information and treatment permission along on all field trips. If needed, include an EpiPen and person trained to use it. (See Chapter 10, "First Aid," p. 132, for more information on the EpiPen.)

Take Nothing but Pictures, Leave Nothing but Footprints

If you concentrate on activities aimed at collecting data rather than specimens at field sites, you protect yourself as well as the environment. Before planning an activity that results in removing something from or irreversibly disturbing the field study area, ask yourself if there is any other reasonable way you could accomplish the same educational goals. Science is more about observing than about collecting, so the less intervention with the observed system the better. So much the better, too, if you and your students can observe without touching. Let the hands be on the instruments rather than on the organisms. That way you minimize the hazards that unknown or unanticipated organisms can pose and you make the fewest changes in the ecosystem you visit. You minimize contacts with potential allergens or infectious agents, and you avoid the inadvertent removal or harming of protected species.

Similarly, plan on carrying out everything you bring into a field site, including used materials, leftover supplies, and trash. Be aware that each outdoor environment has its own, delicately balanced, perhaps unique, ecosystem. For that reason, you should not simply release classroom-raised organisms to the outdoors. They may be completely alien species, unable to survive, or, worse, they may have insufficient predators. The introduction of an alien species can negatively alter an environment forever.

9

Classrooms Without Walls

Field studies reinforce science skills and create memorable experiences that last long after isolated facts have disappeared. With careful planning—in which students can share—you can teach observational and data-collecting skills, applying these to complex, real-world systems.

At the same time, a well-prepared, focused group of students can demonstrate to outsiders what serious education is going on in today's classrooms. So take that first step. Plan your next adventure. Just remember to pack those safety backpacks to take with you.

THE SAVVY SCIENCE TEACHER

Mr. K has an adventuresome spirit. That's why he volunteered to be an exchange teacher in an American middle school. Even though the behaviors and attitudes of his new students were far different than those in his native country, he felt he could share his spirit of adventure safely.

Mr. K's Red Team had studied biomes in science and Asia in social studies. When he announced a trip to the zoo, his class had two distinct reactions: "Yeah, we get out of here" and "Boring! We were there in first grade." Attitude adjustment was in order.

He prepared Red Team for the trip. Groups were assigned specific, quantitative observations at six exhibits: What proportion of a lion's time is spent walking? What is the average swimming speed of penguins? Because they would need data to support their observations, the students drafted an equipment list—watches, cameras, charts and graphs. Using a zoo map, groups planned their routes to allow 15 minutes at each station. They also planned to report to Mr. K at two required checkpoints. Finally, they met with their adult group leader to get approval of their expedition plan.

On the day of the trip, students were excited. Their frenetic body language reflected their feeling of adventure. But by the end of their first observations they had settled into routine and acted as good scientists throughout. Mr. K is planning Red Team's next big adventure.

9

Connections

▶ Adler, D.A., N. Tobin (Illustrator). 1999. *How Tall, How Short, How Faraway.* New York, NY: Holiday House.

▶ Foster, G. W. 1999. *Elementary Mathematics and Science Methods: Inquiry Teaching and Learning.* Belmont, CA: Wadsworth Publishing Co.

▶ Keteyian, L. 2001. A Garden Story. *Science and Children* 39 (3): 22–25.

▶ Robertson, W. C. 2001. *Community Connections for Science Education: Building Successful Partnerships.* Arlington, VA: NSTA Press.

▶ Russell, H. R. 2001. *Ten-Minute Field Trips.* Arlington, VA: NSTA Press.

▶ Kids' Lightning Information and Safety. *www.azstarnet.com/ anubis/zaphome.htm*

9

The Kitchen Sink

A Potpourri of Safety Tips

Ms. M enters school shortly after 7 a.m. On her left arm is a tote bag full of corrected lab notebooks. In her right hand is a bulging briefcase with a copy of the district's sixth grade science learning expectations, several CD-ROMs with software she's been testing at home; a bulletin with the revised district policy on student Internet access; a suggested activity list from Habitat Camp, site of the week-long seventh grade field experience; and the Red Cross manual for the cardiopulmonary resuscitation course she's been taking. There's also a clipboard with reminder notes: "Check photo permission slips for cable television program next week; sign out video camera from the media center; ask school nurse about Tito's dust mite allergies; call Maria's guardian about eyeglasses instead of contacts." On her wrist are a dozen rubber bands for students who come to class with shoulder-length hair.

Middle school teaching isn't just about the curriculum. When students rotate from class to class, minutes are precious. You must plan to structure a class period to everyone's best advantage, anticipating a myriad of issues that will have to be resolved in the course of just one period. Each time you check off an item, two more appear. This chapter is devoted to that list—the small details that can make or break a program.

Middle school students are among the most inventive individuals you will ever meet. Just when you think you've accounted for every possible way a lab activity might require safety instructions, you will find a lab group that has conceived a new way to approach the activity. Most of the topics in this chapter apply not just to safety in science activities but also to safe teaching practices in general. Many of the recommendations have practical application to the everyday lives of your students outside school, making it doubly worth the effort to incorporate safety issues throughout your teaching. Safety should be a universal concern. Do not hesitate to ask for help from your students, fellow teachers, administrators, and parents in making it so.

10

Persistent Problems

Although it is relatively easy to analyze the safety concerns that might be related to a single lab activity, we sometimes take the general conditions of our assigned classroom spaces for granted. We now know the buildings we occupy are not always as healthful an environment as they might be. Asthma, allergies, and other persistent symptoms seem to be on the rise as buildings are made more airtight. Be alert to such signs as lingering coughs, sneezing, eye rubbing, headaches, and lethargy. They may be a signal that some irritant is present in your facility.

The Not-So-Magic Carpet

Carpets have never been recommended for laboratory classrooms. Many middle school classrooms, however, have a great deal of carpet, despite the fact that recent studies have suggested its use in school rooms may create more problems than benefits. If the room you use for lab activities was converted from a regular classroom, there may even be wall-to-wall carpeting.

If possible, request the removal of all carpeting from science rooms. This floor covering may be the source of a host of problems difficult to trace or resolve. The substance most frequently used in science activities is water, both as a chemical reagent and for cleanup. A wet carpet makes an ideal breeding ground for the molds and mildew that are the most frequent and persistent cause of allergies and asthma in a closed environment. The glues and adhesives from newly installed carpet may outgas, causing mild but persistent headaches or dizziness. Besides molds and mildew, infrequently or improperly cleaned carpets can harbor dust mites, dander, and other allergens and disease-causing organisms. Spilled fluids can penetrate to carpet backing and padding, so surfaces that appear clean may be covering contaminated material below. The highly recommended alternative to carpets is nonskid resilient flooring.

If you suspect your classroom carpets are causing health problems and they cannot be removed, request a thorough cleaning with mildew treatment. Make sure the room is ventilated after treatment so the fluids can evaporate quickly. Even with thorough cleaning, some dander cannot be removed from carpets, so classroom pets, mammals in particular, should never be allowed on carpeted floors. The upholstery of old furniture may pose similar problems.

The Class Menagerie

If you have animals or many plants in your room, the food, waste, and soils can harbor mold and spores that last for years in the air of a classroom. Parasitic cysts from animal waste, classroom pets, and dissection specimens can resist all common cleaning agents. Limit the number of plants you keep, and use commercial potting soil. Do not bring animal carcasses into the classroom. (See Chapter 5, "Call of the Wild," p. 65.)

10

Heavy Metal Is More Than Loud Music

Heavy metal and organic compounds can persist in cracks and crevices in flooring and furniture despite regular cleaning. This is a greater problem when a middle school building was once a high school. Many compounds that were used for science activities and cleaning in years past are now known to be hazardous—toxic or carcinogenic. Mercury used in older thermometers and other measuring instruments poses the greatest hazard. Replace all mercury-filled instruments and turn over the old instruments for hazardous waste disposal. If you see traces of spilled mercury in your room, request hazardous waste removal services.

Potable Water

Although most schools have municipal or well water that is tested and safe, some older schools have questionable sources or aging iron/lead piping systems. If your school water is not certified as safe for drinking, make the issue and the reasons for it a science lesson for students. Make sure your students know the nearest source of potable water, and identify it with signs and frequent reminders.

Keeping Clean

The newest cleaning formulas increasingly tout their germ-killing ingredients. It is important to recognize just how many and what kinds of weapons need to be brought to the battle with germs. More often than not, just plain soap and warm water are enough. Sometimes a 70% alcohol solution is sufficient or perhaps a 10% bleach solution is all that is needed. Using cleaners that have antibiotics is neither necessary nor recommended: Science classes need not contribute to the selective evolution of super germs.

In some cases, frequent soap-and-water hand washing by people with sensitive skin may result in chapping and skin breaks that can cause problems of their own. Try substituting the newer alcohol hand cleaning gels. They are made of quick-drying alcohol formulations. Another solution is using disposable nonlatex (e.g., nitrile) gloves. Use and teach the surgeon's technique of removing disposable gloves by flipping them inside out.

Recent changes in federal and some state laws require that schools restrict the amount and types of materials used for cleaning, disinfecting, and pest control. In some cases, parents and others must be notified before certain chemicals are applied. Check to be sure you are not using some cleaning agent or disinfectant material that is banned or restricted from use in school buildings. Use information on the material safety data sheet (MSDS), and check with building administrators and school facilities personnel. A good rule: Use the mildest possible chemical to perform the task.

10

Standard (Universal) Precautions— Typical School Practices

- Never bring blood or blood products into the classroom.
- Always have nonlatex gloves available for use in cases of bleeding.
- Provide sterile gauze pads to the injured individual to cover and hold over the wound.
- Do not interfere in a fight in a manner that could expose you to blood or biting.
- Use approved disinfectants for blood or body fluid spills. To prevent splashing, cover the spill with paper towels or absorbent cloth such as an old T-shirt, then pour the disinfectant over the towels/cloth.
- Use a specially marked disposal container for all materials contaminated with blood and other body fluids.
- All designated personnel who might clean up body fluids should be vaccinated against hepatitis B.

Refer to your school and community health services for more specifics.

First Aid

Topic: first aid/CPR
Go to: www.scilinks.org
Code: SML132

It's reasonable and prudent to be prepared for the unexpected. First aid training courses from the American Red Cross are highly recommended. Most states have Good Samaritan laws that provide liability protection. Check to find the specifics in your state.

An EpiPen or Adrenalin injection can be of critical importance and is easily administered by a properly trained person. Without it, anaphylactic shock from an insect sting could result in a fatality. Although relatively simple to use, it must be administered only by prescription by a nurse or person trained by the prescribing physician. Find out about your district policy, and make sure you or someone else is trained to use an EpiPen.

Standard (Universal) Precautions

In response to hazards associated with bloodborne pathogens, OSHA required the use of Universal Precautions for the handling of human blood. When it was recognized other body fluids might also carry and transmit pathogens, these practices were later expanded to include the handling of any human body fluids and are now called Standard Precautions.

The handling of body fluids such as blood, saliva, and vomitus requires prior training in the proper procedures to protect against transmission of pathogens such as human immunodeficiency virus (HIV) and hepatitis. Hepatitis vaccination is normally recommended if you have these responsibilities. The accepted standard of care is to use Standard Precautions in all instances involving body fluids. Check with your school health officer for specifics on how the Standard Precautions are implemented in your dis-

10

trict. The body fluids from any person should be treated as if they might be infectious—no exceptions.

Use and Disposal of Sharps

Sharps include tools, parts of tools, and broken objects with sharp edges or points that can break the skin and cause cuts or other injuries. Metal blades, broken glass, or plastic with jagged edges are all considered sharps. If you use materials that have sharp points or edges or that can be broken into pieces with points or sharp edges, you must prepare a separate disposal container for them. This container should not be opened or emptied, but rather disposed of intact and then replaced with a new one. Make sure everyone who uses your room or handles your trash knows about the sharps container, uses it, and handles it correctly.

You and your students can easily make sharps disposal containers. You can use a plastic gallon jug or a corrugated box sealed on all sides. Cut a small slot in the container large enough to accept broken or sharp items for disposal. Label the sharps disposal container prominently on all sides. Make sure your custodian will recognize it immediately. If an object with sharp or broken edges is too large for your regular sharps container, make a special one just for that object. Be sure to label it clearly, and place it near the regular sharps container for disposal.

Sharp and pointed instruments can be very tempting for students, so carefully inventory all sharp items distributed for use during class and make sure you collect them all after use. If someone does get cut, be sure to observe Standard Precautions for handling body fluids in treating the blood and wound. (See Chapter 10, p. 132, "Standard Precautions.")

The Latex Connection

Latex has been identified as a serious allergen—causing reactions as simple as rash and irritation and as serious as anaphylactic shock. Common sources of latex in the classroom are in "rubber" gloves, both disposable and nondisposable. Nonlatex (e.g., nitrile) gloves are recommended instead of latex gloves. Rubber tubing and rubber dams may also be made of latex.

Another source of latex in the classroom is in the common balloon. In addition to latex as a potential allergen, these balloons present a choking hazard if students fool around while blowing them up.

Red Means Stop, Green Means Go—Or Do They?

Color blindness, particularly red-green color blindness, is more common than most people suspect. If you use color-coding in organizing your room or activities, particularly if you use red to symbolize a safety warning or precaution, make sure you also include verbal or graphic indicators so color-blind individuals do not miss your meaning or distinction. This sex-linked trait often goes unnoticed even into adulthood until some comic or unfortunate incident makes the effect apparent. It is highly unlikely any boys in your middle school classes realize they are color-blind, even though some may be affected from mildly to severely.

The Scientific Gourmet

Investigations with food and cooking have long been a part of science activities, but these investigations present special problems. They are especially difficult at the middle school level where classrooms are shared and many students use the same desks and work surfaces each day.

No Cooking, No Eating

There are many suggestions for edible science activities in books and curriculum resources. But there should be no eating in a science facility. The hidden dangers that come with consumption of food or drink in a science room or science activity area fall into two categories. First, the area may be contaminated with surprisingly persistent toxins, including heavy metals, organic compounds, molds, and pathogens. In a shared science space, you can never be sure of what materials were there before or how well the space was cleaned. Second, students who are in the habit of eating in a science work space may be tempted to taste a material that is meant for research. The best rule is the most simple: Nothing should be tasted or eaten as part of science lab work. No snacks or food should be eaten in a science room or in the part of the general room where science investigations have taken place.

But what about those motivating experiences that involve foods such as observing changes in popping corn or measuring the calories in peanuts—middle school activities often followed by consuming the products or the leftovers? The best strategy is to move the activity to a different locale—one associated with food preparation and not with science activities, such as the cafeteria or home economics room. Use only nonlab equipment and materials. If this is impossible, then the resulting food should not be eaten. Many science teachers go further and never permit the consumption of any product of a scientific investigation.

Nut Allergies

An increasing number of students and adults have been identified with serious—often life-threatening—allergies to nuts. An allergic reaction may be triggered not only by ingestion but also by proximity to a nut or nut product. If such an allergic individual is present in your class, then you must avoid investigations involving nuts, nut oils, and nut by-products. School authorities may also have to take steps to

10

eliminate these products in breakfast and lunch programs and provide separated eating facilities to ensure there is no exposure from snacks or other foods brought into the classroom or school building. Eliminating peanuts and peanut products from classrooms altogether would be prudent. Confer with the school nurse to get information on all student allergies at the beginning of the year.

Dress of the Day

Dress codes may be controversial in the school in general, but in the science classroom safety takes precedence. Some clothing fashions are just poor choices for science activities.

Begin with the philosophy that the classroom is a "workplace"—an environment where commonsense clothing is required. Loosely hanging, floppy clothing and hanging jewelry are not reasonable. Coats, jackets, hats, and similar loose-fitting, overhanging, and dangling articles should be removed and stored away from work and lab areas. Bare midriffs are not acceptable. Absorbent watchbands and wrist ornaments should be removed. Hair should be tied, pinned, or otherwise secured back behind the shoulders. Backpacks and totes should be stored in lockers or other storage areas. Shoes should have closed toes and be securely tied. No platform shoes or any other footwear that is likely to result in tripping and falling should be worn in a science laboratory. This is a matter of safe practice rather than fashion commentary. And of course, remind the adults (especially aides, interns, and student teachers) to conform to the same dress guidelines.

Piercings pose another problem for the science classroom. No jewelry should hang or protrude from a working scientist. If a student insists a particular piece of jewelry cannot be removed, cover it completely with tape or a bandage.

Combustible Fabrics

Even when you've controlled for the major fashion crazes, you may still have trouble with the fabrics in student clothing. Many are highly flammable and may also melt at relatively low temperatures, causing severe burns and permanent injuries. Ask for help from your local fire department to demonstrate the high flammability of fabrics, especially filmy, gauzy fabrics. Teach students what to do if clothing catches fire. Have kids demonstrate stop, drop, and roll to parents and siblings.

Eyewear

Contact lenses, especially soft contact lenses, can absorb chemical fumes or otherwise trap chemicals in the eye, rendering eyewash ineffective. Contact lenses can be worn with well-fitting safety glasses if there is no risk of exposure to strong chemical fumes. They should not be worn, with or without safety glasses, if there is a risk of exposure to strong chemical fumes or chemical splash. For students, the conditional nature of these warnings can lead to confusion or mistaken practice, so we recommend "contacts out, glasses on" when participating in any activity that requires safety glasses. If students say they don't have regular glasses, confer with the parents or guardians to explain the hazard of contact lens use during science activities and ask them to consult an ophthalmologist.

Many teachers associate eye protection with chemistry activities, but it is also a must in many other circumstances. Any activity that can generate projectiles requires eye protection. That includes dissection, because the preservatives and parts can splash and the instruments are sharp. It includes activities with rubber bands, too. Make sure safety goggles are certified for safety—for splash and/or impact, as appropriate—and are not just the "plant visitor specs." If safety goggles are shared, they must be sterilized after every use, either in an ultraviolet (UV) cabinet or in hot water and detergent or disinfectant, to prevent the spread of conjunctivitis and hepatitis. If your students change classes, it's good to instill in them the habit of dropping their eye protection in the sink with antibacterial soap and water during the end-of-class cleanup time and picking up a pair to rinse as they walk in. Try a sign: Welcome—It's an Eye Protection Day. If an accident happens, have the eyewash clean and ready. (See Chapter 3, "Where Science Happens," p. 23.)

Pregnancies

Although we hate to face the possibility, girls in middle schools become pregnant. We must be conscious of signs of illness and refer any student with possible problems to the proper school counseling or nursing staff. This is especially important in science, where some chemicals—such as formalin or safranin stain—are far more dangerous to pregnant teens than to nonpregnant teens. Since you won't always know if a student is pregnant, the best caution is to avoid completely the use of the chemicals.

10

The Internet Connection

The National Science Education Standards (*National Science Education Standards*, NRC 1996) encourage teachers to go beyond the walls of their classrooms, taking students both virtually and physically into contact with real science. The Internet provides many opportunities, but sites must be screened carefully for accuracy and usefulness. Create a hot list or website where your students can access specific sites. Remember you are responsible for ensuring your students' work on the Internet is carefully designed and supervised to keep them as safe as possible when they venture into this learning environment.

Remember that, unlike formal print publications, the information posted on Internet websites need not be edited or vetted. False, misleading, and downright dangerous information is just as prevalent on the Internet as accurate, up-to-date, and useful information. It is therefore essential that you provide students with carefully structured Internet assignments and that you have screened sites you intend them to use.

Unsupervised exploration is an invitation to disaster. Although most schools have Internet filters in place, it is important to remember that they are not foolproof. Translation: They don't work. Many sites offer potentially dangerous information; not only pornographers but also hate groups, anarchists, and members of cults and fringe groups use the Internet to contact young people.

Make sure your students have clear and appropriately timed assignments. Arrange the monitors so an adult supervisor can see them at all times, and circulate around the room to view all the screens frequently. Check student interactions to make sure they are on task.

Under no circumstances should students be allowed to provide their full names or demographic information on the Internet. E-mails to student pen pals should be screened through the teacher, using first names or pseudonyms. No chat rooms should be allowed, except through certified educational programs. For example, both the National Science Teachers Association, found at www.nsta.org, and the JASON program, found at www.jason.org, offer well-supervised chats with researchers. If you share group pictures of experiments or discoveries on the Internet, identify them by classroom, not by student names. Never put pictures of students in which they are identifiable on the Internet, but back views are all right.

If your district has developed an Internet-use policy and a written contract to be signed by students and parents, be sure you know the policy and follow it carefully. The sample provided is a starting point, but, as with all the samples forms in this book, you should develop one that is aligned with local and state policy and approved by your district's legal counsel.

10

SAMPLE INTERNET-USE GUIDELINES AND CONTRACT

Source: The Brookline Public Schools, Mass.

GUIDELINES

The primary purpose of the Internet connection is educational; therefore, the_____ School(s)

▶ *Takes no responsibility for any information or materials that are transferred through the Internet and requires users to refrain from downloading inappropriate, non-educational material;*

▶ *Will not be liable for the actions of anyone connecting to the Internet through this hook-up. All users shall assume full liability, legal, financial, or otherwise, for their actions;*

▶ *Makes no guarantees, implied or otherwise, regarding the reliability of the data connection. The _____ Schools shall not be liable for any loss or corruption of data resulting from use of the Internet connection;*

▶ *Reserves the right to examine all data stored in computers or on disks which are the property of the _____ Schools to ensure that users are in compliance with these regulations;*

▶ *Strongly condemns the illegal acquisition and/or distribution of software, otherwise known as pirating. Any users transferring such files through the Internet, and any whose accounts are found to contain such illegal files, may have their accounts permanently revoked;*

▶ *Reminds all users that when they use the Internet, they are entering a global community, and any actions taken by them will reflect upon the school system as a whole. As such, we expect that all users will behave in an ethical and legal manner;*

▶ *Reserves the right to change or modify these rules at any time without notice.*

CONTRACT

I, _____, agree:

To abide by all rules which are listed in the _____ Schools Guidelines for Internet Use;

That the primary purpose of the _____ Schools Internet connection is educational;

10

That the use of the Internet is a privilege, not a right;

Not to participate in the transfer of inappropriate or illegal materials, including the intellectual property of others through the _____ Schools Internet connection;

Not to allow other individuals to use my account for Internet activities, nor will I give anyone my password.

I understand that inappropriate behavior may lead to penalties, which may include discipline, revocation of account, or legal action.

I realize that there are inappropriate and possibly offensive materials available to those who use the Internet, and the undersigned hereby releases the _____ Schools from any liability or damages that may result from the viewing of, or contact with, such materials.

Signed:_____ Date:_____

Parents must sign if the user is under eighteen years of age.

I, _____, the parent/guardian of the above, agree to accept all financial and legal liabilities which may result from my son's/daughter's use of the _____ Schools Internet connection.

Signed:_____ Date:_____

MY INTERNET CONTRACT

I, _____, promise to obey all school policies and rules about the Internet. I will only use search engines for appropriate school assignments. I will avoid inappropriate sites. I will not join chat rooms or use a personal e-mail account at school. I will not download material or change the settings on school computers. I understand that violation of these rules may result in discipline and loss of all computer privileges.

_____(Student)   _____(Parents)

10

Picture This

Public schools are required to protect students' privacy rights. One area that often becomes an issue is photographing them.

At the beginning of each year, make sure district-approved parental consent documents have been obtained and filed before any photographs are taken. Before releasing any photographs to an outside entity, make sure that you have the clear written consent of the parent or guardian and that you are following district rules.

Special circumstances may make even standard photo releases inappropriate. Students are sometimes the subjects of custody disputes, and photos can endanger their safety. Photos of disabled students and students in special needs classrooms might inadvertently subject a child to unwanted public attention. Photos of students in certain disciplinary or instructional situations might imply some negative connotations. When in doubt, ask the parents again.

Privacy vs Public Access

Your students and their parents have a reasonable expectation of privacy while students are in your care. They rely on your judgment. Reporters, researchers, and even police agency representatives do not have the right to question students without parent consent. One major exception—in almost every state, representatives of agencies responsible for child protective services and prevention of child abuse may question students in the presence of a school official without the permission of their parents.

Some of the most difficult privacy issues arise with divorced and separated parents whose rights depend on specific arrangements ordered by the courts. One of the key goals of effective schools is to be welcoming to parents and to their participation in their children's education. But in cases where noncustodial parents are barred by court order from

SAMPLE CONSENT AND RELEASE FORM

Source: The Brookline Public Schools, Mass.

Dear Parents:

Reporters from newspapers, magazines, and television often approach us to interview, photograph, and/or videotape our students. These members of the press are often motivated to make these requests because of the nature of our instructional programs. Occasionally they will simply want a picture of children coming to school on the opening day. In addition, we may have textbook companies request permission to photograph a classroom at work to include in a publication.

We do not allow any children to be interviewed/photographed, and/or videotaped by the media and/or school personnel for publicity or newspapers without having your permission. I am asking that you indicated below whether you are willing to grant such permission. Please complete the tear-off and return it to your child's classroom teacher. Thank you for your assistance.

(Signature) _____

CONSENT AND RELEASE

I hereby grant [ ] or withhold [ ] permission for photographs, videotaping, and/or interviews of my child _____ to be used in school publications and/or outside media during the time she/he attends the _____ Schools.

Parent/guardian signature:_____

Address:_____

Date:_____

(Reprinted with permission of the Brookline Public Schools.)

10

contact with their children or participation in decisions concerning their children, the schools, and you as an employee, must comply. As a teacher, you may be directly approached by parents whose access to their children has been restricted by the courts. Your school administrator can advise you of any precautions you must take regarding visits from noncustodial parents.

Many schools allow students to produce newspapers and videos for cable channels. When a regular student news or weather program is produced, you may be able to provide parents with a blanket permission slip for participation. If a special topic is planned, parents should again be asked for consent. This includes assignments where students are creating videos for science projects.

E.T. Phone Home—or E-Mail

Teachers need telephones and e-mail capability in their classrooms for ordinary communications as well as for emergencies. Parents need to be partners in your work with their children, and communication is critical to this partnership. The better teachers and parents know each other, the better they can work together to support students and ensure their safety at home and at school. At the very least, you need a functioning means of calling for help or reporting a problem instantly. Keep a log of your calls and other communications to document your ongoing efforts to keep everyone informed.

Crisis Prevention and Response

Promises to Keep

Provide opportunities for informal conversation with your students, but do not promise secrecy. You need to assure students you will respect their private communications with you but not at the expense of exercising your judgment in protecting them and others.

As the all-too-common headlines of school violence and crises show, this book could never describe everything needed for security. The most effective safety factor in a school is the staff. A caring, watchful group of adults can spot potential problems before they are even imagined.

Keep the door open, but do not force students to talk about untoward and anxiety-provoking events. Middle school students often appear far more sophisticated and adult than they actually are. Hiding anxiety and fear from adults and peers is common practice for these very young adults.

There is a significant body of evidence to support the idea of middle school houses or teams.

10

Organizing a larger school into smaller, personalized groups in which everyone knows everyone else is a valuable safety system in itself. If this is possible in your school, consider it.

Science teachers in particular can play key roles in crisis prevention. You have many opportunities to work with students in informal settings. When you do group work, you have a good opportunity to observe and hear students' attitudes emerge. Put up your antennas for signs of troubled students. Report your observations to administrators and counselors. Follow up in writing. Never ignore threats or warning signs from students, assuming they are just kidding.

Keep your room well organized and clutter-free. That way you are more likely to be aware of items that have been removed from your room or unusual items or bags left there. Items you cannot identify as harmless should be reported and not handled. Do not ask students to bring large collections of items or unusually complex materials from home. This adds to clutter and ambiguity.

Keep your room locked when you aren't present. This is a challenge, especially during all-too-short changes of class. But you may be held liable for what happens in your classroom when you are not there.

Do not send students on errands outside the building or assign them to work anywhere away from your direct supervision and sight unless there is another trained individual to supervise their work. Hall pass excursions should be brief and purposeful. Independent project work should be scheduled within view of an adult at all times.

Begin and end class with a regular routine that accounts for everyone and everything. You can ask groups to take attendance and help with the distribution of supplies. At the end of the activity, these or other groups can check that everyone has returned all supplies equipment and that cleanup has occurred. Start and end the period with calm and a sense of purpose.

Plan for the worst so you can securely enjoy the best of times. With your fellow staff members and the support of the administration, create and train crisis response teams to respond to medical and psychological crises, threats and acts of violence, and the range of circumstances that require immediate action for the welfare and safety of students and others in the schools. Such teams should plan for emergencies and ensure that individuals are trained and available to provide first aid, psychological support, physical security, and public information. Include and maintain regular contact with representatives from state and local agencies that provide assistance and emergency response—police and fire departments, community mental health agencies, local hospitals, the state health department.

10

Planning for the Future

Don't wait until September to make plans for the coming year. When your principal begins to discuss next year's assignments, schedule an appointment to consider these priorities:

▶ *Class size:* Although additional facilities and equipment can make science safer for larger groups of students, the number of students that can be effectively and safely taught in an active investigative science program has a limit. There is a very high, positive correlation between class size and accident rate no matter how good the facilities. Although experts disagree on an absolute limit, statistics show accidents increase dramatically as classes increase beyond 20 to 24 students or when the space is less than 4 m² per student.

▶ *Scheduling:* Preparing for science activities takes thought and time. Equipment must be inventoried and checked for correct and safe functioning. Surfaces must be cleaned before and after messy activities. This kind of preparation cannot be done during a five-minute break or while students are doing seat work. Preparation time needs to be scheduled rather than squeezed in, especially if you are team teaching, need to share space, or move from one location to another. Request firmly that you have similar classes scheduled in sequence, with a prep period between major subject changes.

▶ *Security:* In some states, two exits are required for science rooms. If you state does not require two exits for a science classroom, request a room with two exit doors that is not in a heavy-traffic area or near a major school entrance. Check for a good ventilation system and for good communication with the office. Get a phone, and make sure it works. If you suspect old copies of your classroom key are floating around, ask for your room to be rekeyed. Keys to science storage areas and rooms solely dedicated to science instruction should be unique. These rooms should not be accessible with keys used to enter regular classrooms or common areas. Air from science storage areas should be vented directly to the outside.

Adolescent Wit and Wisdom

Those of us who have spent years with middle school students would not exchange our positions for any other. The middle school imagination presents us with surprises and challenges every day. Middle school students are emergent thinkers, having absorbed enough information and matured enough from concrete operational stages of development to begin to apply concepts and synthesize new ideas. Lacking the inhibition of their older counterparts in high school they freely speculate, dare, and challenge authority. Those who best survive the rigors of middle school teaching—and love it—have learned to keep a sense of humor and delight in the spontaneity of middle schoolers. When you think you are about to lose your own mind, remember to laugh and enjoy the wonders of the middle school mind.

10

THE SAVVY SCIENCE TEACHER

It was only February, but Ms. N was already exhausted. First there was that schedule: first and fourth hour Earth science, second and fifth physical science, third hour life science, and no prep until sixth. By midyear she had identified two severely disabled students and several with special needs not previously identified. Because of all the different sciences, Ms. N was switching classrooms almost every period with no time between, often finding a surprisingly messy room when she walked in to try and begin class.

She considered resigning at the end of the year, but, when she realized how much she loved teaching, she decided instead to change things. First, she spoke with three colleagues who taught different subjects. They were experiencing the same exhaustion, but also did not want to throw in the towel just yet. Together they brainstormed ideas and solicited the opinions and support of others in the school. By May, they had a proposal for the equally exhausted principal.

Divide the teaching staff into clusters, assign four teachers to each cluster—one each in English, social studies, math, and science—and give these teachers all the students of the same grade level. Each cluster would meet with guidance and special needs staff to divide students into classes based on information about the needs and characteristics of the students. Some classes with severely disabled students would have fewer students and a co-teacher. Other classes would have students with similar special needs in them. Planning periods would be arranged so at least two persons in a cluster would have planning periods at the same time and teachers teaching simultaneously could regroup students across disciplines for special projects.

Because they would no longer have to prepare science lessons for all three grade levels, each science teacher would be assigned a classroom so projects and materials could be left in place between classes. Field trips could be planned within clusters so all four subject-area teachers could match fieldwork to class work and not have to plan around some students' missing some activities while others remained in class.

A two-week summer planning workshop would give everyone a chance to work out more of the specifics. September would be upon them before they knew it, but this time everyone looked forward to the new year.

10

Connections

▶ American Chemical Society and ACS Board—Council Committee on Chemical Safety. 2001. *Chemical safety for teachers and their supervisors.* Washington, DC: American Chemical Society. Available in PDF format at *membership.acs.org/c/ccs/pubs/chemical_safety_manual.pdf*

▶ Sprenger, M. B. 2002. *Becoming a "wiz" at brain-based teaching: How to make every year your best year.* Thousand Oaks, CA: Corwin Press Inc.

10

Live Long and Prosper

And Remember You Are Responsible

Consider the changes. Yesterday's seventh and eighth graders are today's middle schoolers, no longer children but instead burgeoning young adults. Physical puberty comes early and, encouraged by the media, that emotional time of wanting to be an adult even sooner. Teachers race to keep up with what their students experience outside school. Everything has changed, yet everything remains the same. You, the teacher, remain responsible for everyone and for everything in your classroom, an awesome responsibility—and a world of opportunity.

Four Ps for Professionals

You are the professional. Your responsibilities include more than the education of your students. Even though you may see them only one period a day, you act in loco parentis—in a legal sense, in place of parents for the students assigned to you. You can assume these responsibilities because you

▸ **P**repare: Your formal education and studies leading to qualification and certification to teach are just the beginning of your professional training and development. You constantly keep up to date with continuing education by joining and participating in professional organizations and by reading journals and research reports in education, instructional strategies, and subject areas. You make yourself thoroughly familiar with the learning expectations and standards set by federal, state, and local authorities, and take the time to analyze and compare them to other sources of information—recommendations of professional organizations, research data, and your own knowledge and training. You make sure you read and understand all school policies and procedures that relate to your duties and responsibilities—reviewing and filing new information and bulletins that update manuals and other official documents.

11

- **P**lan: You take the time to consider what you are required to teach and the best strategies to ensure your students can learn effectively and safely. You write out your plans, not just so others can read them, but so you can review and critique them yourself before you begin the lesson and after it is over. If you have interns, student teachers, aides, parent volunteers, or any other assistants, you determine how best to train them to work effectively and safely with you and your students. You think ahead about the learning styles, maturity, and behavior of each of your students and determine the best way to work with their strengths and their limitations.

- **P**revent: You take the time to assess hazards and review procedures for accident prevention. You teach and review safety procedures with every student and adult for every potential hazard. You post safety signs and keep copies of safety information. If you detect safety hazards you cannot mitigate, you put your concerns and requests for assistance or changes in writing to the appropriate supervisor and do not use the defective equipment until the hazard is mitigated.

- **P**rotect: You check your facilities for the presence and accessibility of correctly specified and correctly operating safety equipment and protective devices. You count the protective devices you have, such as safety glasses or aprons, to ensure you have enough for everyone who needs them. You demonstrate and instruct students and helpers on the proper use of safety equipment and protective gear. You keep records of safety lessons and instructions to ensure no one has missed getting the information. You insist on the use of protective devices by everyone in the room, including yourself and all visitors.

Broadening Your Definition of Safety

As classroom teacher and science teacher, you need to consider safety as broadly as possible. The chapters of this book are not intended to be an exhaustive manual of everything you must do or know to ensure safe science investigations. Rather, they are meant to sharpen your observational skills so you recognize the issues and circumstances that require your attention to and planning for conducting science inquiry safely. No single book or series of books can anticipate all the safety issues that can arise in an active science program. Nor can any book, this one included, anticipate what new information and technology will render the advice given inaccurate or incorrect. It is the habit of observing and thinking about science lessons with common sense and safety in mind that will keep you and your students safe.

A Diversity of Needs

Your students probably are quite diverse in their needs, their abilities, and their prior experiences. In most middle schools, your roster will include students with a high level of self-control and some with almost none. You must take these issues into ac-

11

count in your planning and your activities. You can still do hands-on activities, but you must choose them wisely and structure them for success.

Remember that accommodation and modification are your legal and professional responsibilities. You cannot delegate them to the special education department, nor can the special education department leave you to your own devices. Have you prepared for special physical needs, special educational needs, and special behavioral needs? It is your responsibility to read individual education plans (IEPs) and be prepared to meet their requirements. Your special education personnel are obligated to help explain IEP goals and objectives when you ask.

Other students may have needs identified under Section 504 of the Americans with Disabilities Act. Even though they are not special education students, they are entitled to modifications and these are a general education legal responsibility.

Look at Me—Talk to Me

Educational leaders often describe learners as visual, auditory, or kinesthetic. But during the middle school years, the predominant mode of learning is social. You will find the greatest success with cooperative learning in grades 5 through 8.

Science activities are usually designed for students to work freely and cooperatively in an interactive setting. When students work in pairs or small groups, you have the opportunity to observe. How well do they work in groups? Are leadership qualities emerging? Are some of your quieter students finally becoming animated and engaged? On the other hand, is someone exceptionally quiet or sad or unable to handle anger effectively? Are there signs of a possible pregnancy? Do you have students who are always left out or picked on? Use these opportunities to get a better picture of the individuals in your class. As a first-line observer, you are often in the best position to know if a student needs nonacademic help. Reach out, talk, and share your observations with parents and with professionals who may provide additional assistance.

Volunteer Help

Many hands make light work and, often, better science education. But adult volunteers can be a mixed blessing in a busy classroom. If you have regular or occasional helpers and volunteers, you bear the ultimate responsibility for their actions, so make sure you have planned sufficient time to train and instruct them. Many municipalities also require security and criminal background checks on every person who will come in contact with students. Make sure you know the rules and follow them strictly.

Substitute Teachers, Interns, and Student Teachers

The actions of substitute teachers, interns, and student teachers in your classroom are also part of your responsibility. They are considered to be implementing your plans, your rules, and your instructions. Unless you are certain these people are able and qualified to conduct an activity safely and properly, do not plan active investigation

11

for times you are not present. Keep a separate set of lesson plans that can be substituted for science lab activities if you should be absent unexpectedly. Do not ask your intern to be your substitute.

Guests and Others

You also need to safeguard yourself and your students from well-meaning—or not-so-well-meaning—guests or intruders. Investigative science activities usually generate more excitement and more physical movement than most other activities, so it's best to avoid adding guests to these activities.

> ### Name Tags
> Many schools issue name tags when a visitor checks in. A possible security precaution is using smiley face stickers that stay the original color for one day but change color the next day.

In some schools, surprise guests and observers are commonplace. If this is the case, be sure all such people are first cleared by the school administration. All visitors should check in with the school office. This provides the school with a list of who is entering the building and gives visitors an opportunity to receive a warm welcome and assistance in finding the person or location they need. On signing in, they should be issued a dated visitor name tag before proceeding onto the campus. This procedure is particularly important if your class includes a student involved in a dispute about custody or guardianship.

If visitors attend a class when all or some students are engaged in science activities, make sure they are made aware of all safety rules and practices beforehand. You may even want to use a visit as an opportunity to review the rules with your students. You can briefly ask your students to explain the rules to the visitor.

You must be aware of anyone who enters your classroom. Keep doors that open directly to the outside locked from the inside and make sure your students know they should not open the door except with your permission.

Warm Welcome

For some schools, asking all guests to sign in may be a new concept. The school has always been a welcoming environment with an open door policy. No one wants to lose that spirit or let changing times send us into a bunker mentality. Asking all visitors to sign in does not have to change the ambience of the school. In the last analysis, registering your presence is just a courteous thing to do. And the person noting the registration can extend a warm welcome. If a regular routine of meeting and greeting is established, it enables everyone to feel welcome and ensures everyone is treated equally.

Sometimes school personnel may hesitate to ask or remind a parent or frequent visitor to sign in at the office and to bring a written okay from the office if the student is to be dismissed early. Statistically, a problem situation is more likely to result from the actions of someone well known to everyone and familiar with the school than from the actions of a stranger. In one case, a student's mother came to the classroom door and asked to speak to her son. The science teacher knew the mother well and readily agreed, but the teacher didn't know there was a custody dispute. The student didn't come back: His mother kidnapped him and took him to another state. Don't be shy about the rules.

CLASSROOM GUESTS

You are responsible for the conduct of everyone who enters your classroom—students as well as assistants and visitors.

▸ Be sure you are aware of everyone who enters, who they are, and whether they have a legitimate reason for being there.

▸ If you have a classroom door that opens directly to the outside, make sure that it can only be opened from the inside and students understand it may be opened only by or with the permission of an adult inside the room.

▸ During science lab activities that involve special techniques or safety precautions, admit only those who have been adequately instructed in and who are prepared to follow safe procedures. This includes supervisors and other observers. They should understand they should come for the entire sequence of instruction or return at another time.

▸ Screen and prepare all anticipated guests. For adult visitors, including volunteers, you need to make sure that all required security and criminal offender record information (CORI) checks have been made prior to the visit. You may need to explain the process and gain permission to start the checks.

▸ If you are planning to have guest speakers, make sure you have thoroughly planned for their presentations and all safety issues have been addressed.

Legal Responsibilities

In today's litigious society, you cannot prevent a lawsuit from being filed. No matter how unreasonable complaints are, our legal system provides the opportunity for people to take them to court. Well-insured schools may be viewed as having "deep pockets" and become targets of frivolous suits. There are, however, many things that you can do to prevent being found at fault or liable.

11

The Jargon

If an accident occurs, people like to try and fix blame. It is common practice to sue everyone with any connection to the event just to find out which charge can be made to stick. Malpractice attorneys litigate matters of professional misfeasance, nonfeasance, and malfeasance. Here are some simplified definitions:

> *Misfeasance:* Performance of a lawful action in an illegal or improper manner. In a science activity, this might result from using an incorrect chemical for an experiment or too much of the correct chemical. It might include selecting an activity that is inappropriate for the students to whom it was assigned or providing incorrect instructions.. The further you deviate from the recommended district curriculum, the greater the risk you take on for yourself.

> *Nonfeasance:* Omission or failure to do what ought to be done. This could include failure to warn students of safety hazards, to provide eye protection or fire equipment, or to post a standard fire drill exit procedure. If you had eye protection available, but did not make sure your students were using the protection when needed, this could also be considered an omission with liability. Being out of your room when your students are in class can create a nonfeasance liability. If students you are responsible for are working in an alcove, a hall, or some part of the room where you cannot see and supervise them, you could have a nonfeasance problem.

> *Malfeasance:* Intentional wrongdoing, deliberate violation of law or standard, or mismanagement of responsibilities. Ignorance is no excuse. If there is governing law or regulation, or local written policy, you are responsible for knowing about it and conforming. Many states have benchmarks or standards that include safety precautions and lessons. These can have the effect of law even though there is no penalty statute. For example, an adopted state standard may require that you teach some safety procedure but neglect to specify a penalty if you do not. In the event of an accident that might have been prevented with the safety procedure, your failure to teach the procedure may not result in a criminal charge against you but it could be construed as malfeasance for which you could be found liable.

> *Tort:* A wrong you do to someone. If you give students the wrong instructions or fail to provide appropriate safe instructions for performing an activity and the activity results in accident or injury, your action is a tort.

The Best Defense

Sounds intimidating? Perhaps, but you can reduce your exposure to these liabilities dramatically by making safe practice a habit. Here are some tips:

> Document your preparation for safety. Subscribe to journals, read books, and take classes to keep up to date.

> As part of your lesson plans and records, document safety lessons and make sure

11

you keep records of follow-up with safety lessons for students who are absent. Keep records of rules given to students and records of disciplinary action with rules violators.

- Do not leave the premises when you are responsible for students. And do not permit students to work where they are out of your sight and supervision.

- Put your safety needs in writing. Don't just complain: Explain why equipment and maintenance needs are necessary. Follow up on your requests. Don't stop until the situation is corrected. Do not engage in any activity involving a reported safety hazard until the hazard is mitigated.

- If you are facing potential litigation, make sure you have the advice, and possibly the presence, of an attorney who represents your interests before making any statements to anyone else. Consult your teachers' association as well as the administration.

Documents to Keep Up To Date

- District policy manuals and all subsequent policy communications
- State and local curriculum guides
- Lesson plan book
- Attendance and grade book—with correlations to the lesson plan book and records of safety lessons for each individual student
- Inventory of materials and equipment
- Maintenance requests
- Purchase requisitions
- Records and notes of professional development activities.

Insurance

Lawsuits are expensive even if they are dismissed or you are found not to be responsible. You probably have some insurance that covers you for basic liability. But it can cost tens of thousands of dollars just to get a nuisance suit in front of a judge so you can have it dismissed. Before that time, there will be accusations, investigations, and depositions. That's why insurance is vital.

Begin by investigating what coverage you already have. Most school systems have errors and omissions coverage for the institution and its employees. This will cover mistakes. Some states require districts to indemnify and hold harmless their teachers, but policies and regulations may have exemptions and exclusions. Find out what the exceptions are. Insurance policies generally exclude any action that violates the law, and that can be the "Catch-22." If the law says you must teach the fire drill procedure or prohibits the use of alcohol burners, you may find yourself without insurance coverage if you violate the law. Most district policies cover employees, but they may not cover consultants, volunteers, or visitors. You would not be covered for a job in which you were "moonlighting," such as working as a scout leader or curriculum consultant. Check.

11

You may have liability insurance through your union or professional association. In general, these policies will cover the preliminary costs of a lawsuit. They will get you a lawyer quickly, separate from the one that represents the district, and get you preliminary advice. But many of these policies exclude any punitive damages, so the cost of your lawyer may be covered but not the biggest part of a future settlement.

Many teachers carry extra professional coverage through their homeowner's or renter's policy. You can obtain an umbrella policy to extend coverage and back up other liability policies you may have. Your coverage might be a rider for professional liability on an existing policy, usually at very little additional cost. Extra coverage is highly recommended.

Take Heart

With all this talk of litigation and liability you may be asking, "Is inquiry worth it?" With absolute confidence, we say, "Yes." When you take time to prepare for safely conducting an active investigative science program, you not only assist your students in answering the questions on their next test, but you also prepare your students to answer future questions we have yet to imagine. Your habit of conducting work thoughtfully and safely becomes the model for the conduct of your students at home and in their future endeavors. As the first teacher in space, Christa McAuliffe, so elegantly put it, we touch the future when we teach.

THE SAVVY SCIENCE TEACHER

Ms. L was surprised at being asked to report to the office to meet with the legal counsel to the school department. It seems that a student in her third period science class had started a fire at home by lighting a magnesium strip embedded in a plastic cup filled with ammonium dichromate. He thought he was making a model volcano, but his experiment got out of control when the curtains caught fire. The student ended up in the hospital to have his burns treated.

Because he was an avid science student and in Ms. L's Earth science class, his parents were blaming Ms. L and the schools for giving him access to the idea and the materials. The school department attorney asked Ms. L what she knew about his accident. She explained that the ammonium dichromate volcano was an outdated and dangerous demo that neither she nor other up-to-date science teachers were using anymore, so she knew the idea could not have come from her. Well, but how about the material—could the student have gotten it from her storeroom? Ms. L said she was sure he had not, but asked for time to check.

As soon as she returned to her room, Ms. L called the teachers' association representative as well as her own insurance agent to let them know what was transpiring. Thanks to excellent record keeping, Ms. L was able to provide the school's legal staff with records of a major chemical clean-out she had arranged just the year before. The hazardous waste removal manifest showed that a 500-gram container of ammonium dichromate had been taken away. The supply order records and up-to-date MSDS files showed nothing more dangerous than household bleach was present in the middle school.

Two days later, the student's uncle, a scientist, admitted to giving the student the materials and telling him how to put together the ill-fated experiment.

11

Conclusion

Teaching is an incredibly complex process. You make dozens of instructional decisions each hour. You manage an environment, a curriculum, and a community of learners. Sometimes the details can become so daunting you must allocate time to refocus.

Safety issues are that way, too. This book has presented 11 chapters of ideas, warnings, and potential hazards. To relate these ideas to reality, we have included anecdotes—some almost verbatim and some composites—of actual experiences of teachers and supervisors. They are meant to illustrate the risks and the opportunities in the familiar environment of your classroom.

These ideas are aimed at sharpening your perceptions and raising your antennae. If they've dampened your enthusiasm for laboratory and field investigation, please look again. The principles of each chapter are positive, constructive, and practical and should make your job easier rather than harder. Here's a review:

1 Setting the Scene

▶ Introduce exploration sequentially, one skill at a time, gradually increasing the complexity of tasks and the length of investigation time.

▶ Model the behaviors of professional scientists as you teach responsibility and organization.

▶ Have students become your partners in safety procedures so safe work habits become second nature.

▶ Make administrators and facilities staff part of your safety team. Educate them about the conditions and facilities needed to teach science safely.

▶ Reinforce science safety with strategically located signs, posters, and videos produced by students.

2 Communities of Learners

▶ Plan science activities that are accessible to all students.

▶ Eliminate barriers in your room by removing clutter and freeing up space.

▶ Communicate your needs for support to modify your program for special needs students.

▶ Minimize the potential for disruptive behavior with shorter and more specific tasks.

- Request support staff and aides for students who need them, and plan time to train these assistants.

- Investigate adaptive equipment and technologies with consultants and district support staff.

3 Where Science Happens

- Conduct science activities in facilities that provide adequate space and ventilation for safety.

- Provide hot and cold running water and soap in science activity areas.

- Select stable, but easily rearranged, furniture, and provide unobstructed flat work surfaces.

- Ensure safety equipment, such as fire extinguishers, fire blankets, and eyewashes, is operational and accessible.

- Make sure electrical service and wiring to your room are well maintained, provide sufficient amperage, and include ground fault interrupter protection.

4 Finders Keepers

- Provide ample open storage to encourage students to obtain and return simple science supplies easily and safely.

- Include enough locked storage, inaccessible to students, for valuable and fragile supplies and equipment as well as materials too hazardous for direct student access.

- Use locked cabinets specifically planned for storage of chemicals.

- Keep incompatible chemicals separated—arrange storage by chemical properties, not by alphabetical order.

- Make sure chemical inventories are accurate, updated, and regularly reviewed.

- Maintain material safety data sheets (MSDS) for every product—one set in the office and one set in your classroom.

- Prepare materials and supplies for science activities in an adequately sized, ventilated, and well-lit preparation space away from student and other traffic.

- Clear out excess supplies, equipment, and furniture regularly as a vital part of safe practice.

5 Lively Science

▶ Maintain living cultures to provide students with opportunities for activities involving observation and care of living organisms and biological systems.

▶ Choose organisms appropriate for the space and time you have to devote to them and the behavior and maturity of your students. Never opt for headlines over good science.

▶ Begin with simple organisms—plants and invertebrates—before trying to maintain more complex and difficult ones.

▶ Never bring wild or feral animals into the classroom.

▶ Avoid organisms that are toxic or highly allergenic.

▶ Inform students and parents of your cultures and be aware of unusual allergies.

▶ Do not release or plant nonnative species in the open environment.

6 Modern Alchemy

▶ Emphasize careful process skills over drama.

▶ Build responsibility gradually.

▶ Use microscale experiments for safety and to encourage careful observation.

▶ Choose less toxic and dangerous options over traditional labs now known to be hazardous.

▶ Maintain a minimal quantity and variety of chemicals—less is better.

▶ Require the use of appropriate safety equipment by all persons—students and adults—at all times.

7 Striking Gold

▶ Rocks and minerals are hard, sharp, and heavy. Teach students safe procedures for moving heavy objects and using tools before beginning activities.

▶ Never allow tasting of specimens.

▶ Keep students away from contaminated soils and insist on proper hand washing.

▶ Never permit direct observation of the sun.

▶ Review rules and procedures prior to field studies.

8 Falling for Science

▶ Become familiar with and follow the guidelines for use of all school equipment.

▶ Use light and sound experiments to teach students how to prevent damage to eyes and ears.

▶ Make sure all electrical connections are safe and conform to code.

▶ Plan ahead so your room won't have physical barriers such as loose cords and other tripping and falling hazards.

The Great Outdoors

9

▶ Link field trips and field studies to curriculum goals.

▶ Preview the site and abutting properties before planning your field study.

▶ Determine proper clothing and footwear for the site and activities planned.

▶ Meet with cooperating resource people to plan activities.

▶ Orient and train all chaperones in your planned activities and in safety precautions.

The Kitchen Sink

10

▶ Minimize the use of carpets and upholstered furniture to reduce the growth and harboring of dust mites, mold spores, and other allergens.

▶ Regularly and carefully clean living cultures in the room.

▶ Check for the presence of heavy metal contamination from prior activities—remove and correctly dispose of all mercury and mercury-based instruments.

▶ Review clothing, covering, and eyewear for laboratory work.

▶ Ensure proper supervision in using the Internet.

▶ Obtain proper consent forms before photographing students.

▶ Do not prepare food or eat in science activity areas.

▶ Prepare with first aid training, crisis response training, and regular communication with parents.

▶ Plan with others for small class sizes, scheduling, and adequate space and materials for an active science program

▶ Make safety and security a significant concern of everyone.

Live Long and Prosper

▶ Prepare, plan, prevent, and protect.

▶ Become familiar with your school policies and with federal, state, and local laws.

▶ Document everything you do.

▶ Assess your safety lessons and keep good records.

▶ Take responsibility to supervise and train your assistants and volunteers.

▶ Make sure you are adequately protected with liability insurance.

References

Adler, D. A., N. Tobin (Illustrator). 1999. *How tall, how short, how faraway*. New York, NY: Holiday House.

American Association for the Advancement of Science. 1991. *Barrier free in brief: Laboratories and classrooms in science and engineering*. Washington, DC: American Association for the Advancement of Science.

American Chemical Society and ACS Board—Council Committee on Chemical Safety. 2001. *Chemical safety for teachers and their supervisors*. Washington, DC: ACS. Available in PDF format at http://membership.acs.org/c/ccs/pubs/chemical_safety_manual.pdf

Biehle, J., L. Motz, and S. West. 1999. *NSTA guide to school science facilities*. Arlington, VA: NSTA Press.

Flinn Scientific Catalog/Reference Manual. 2002. Batavia, IL: Flinn Scientific, Inc. See www.flinnsci.com/

Foster, G. W. 1999. *Elementary mathematics and science methods: Inquiry teaching and learning*. Belmont, CA: Wadsworth Publishing Co.

Hallowell, E. M., and J. J. Ratey. 1995. *Driven to distraction*. New York: Pantheon Books.

Keteyian, L. 2001. A garden story. *Science and children* 39 (3): 22–25.

Levine, M. 2002. *A mind at a time*. New York: Simon & Schuster.

Lowery, L., ed. 2000. Appendix C in *NSTA pathways to the science standards—elementary school edition*. Arlington, VA: NSTA Press.

McCullough, J., and R. McCullough. 2000. *The role of toys in teaching physics*. College Park, MD: American Association of Physics Teachers.

Merck & Co., Inc. 2001. *The Merck Index, thirteenth edition*. Rahway, NJ: The Merck Publishing Group. See www.merck.com for CD-ROM and online versions.

National Research Council. 1996. *National science education standards*. Washington, DC: National Academy Press. Online version at *www.nap.edu/books/0309053269/html/index.html*

Reese, K. M. 1985. *Teaching chemistry to physically handicapped students*. Washington, DC: American Chemical Society.

Robertson, W. C. 2001. *Community connections for science education: Building successful partnerships*. Arlington, VA: NSTA Press.

Roy, K., P. Markow, and J. Kaufman. 2001. *Safety is elementary: The new standard for safety in the elementary science classroom.* Natick, MA: The Laboratory Safety Institute. See *www.labsafety.org* for additional information.

Russell, H. R. 2001. *Ten-minute field trips.* Arlington, VA: NSTA Press.

Sarquis, M. 2000. *Building student safety habits for the workplace.* Middletown, OH: Terrific Science Press.

Sprenger, M. B. 2002. *Becoming a "wiz" at brain-based teaching: How to make every year your best year.* Thousand Oaks, CA: Corwin Press Inc.

Wood, C. G. 1995. *Safety in school science labs.* Natick, MA: Kaufman and Associates.

Websites

Kids' Lightning Information and Safety. *www.azstarnet.com/anubis/zaphome.htm*

Science Education for Students with Disabilities promotes science for students with disabilities. *www.as.wvu.edu/~scidis/organizations/index.html*

Material safety data sheet links:

Links to most manufacturers' sites: *www.msdsprovider.net/Site/msdsprovider.nsf/about*

Cornell University: *msds.pdc.cornell.edu/msdssrch.asp*

Fisher Scientific: *www.fishersci.com*

Vermont Safety Information Resources, Inc.: *siri.uvm.edu/msds*

Appendix A

Chemicals to Go—Candidates for Disposal

The chemicals in the following table were once used in programs and demonstrations. They now are generally considered too hazardous to store and use in middle school programs. You should check the materials you have in your classroom and stockroom. Anything you do not need for your program should be removed. If your program requires any of the chemicals in this table, you should review the hazards involved, and make sure you have the expertise, training, facilities, protective equipment, and sufficiently mature students to ensure the educational benefits outweigh the risks. Consider replacing these chemicals with a safer alternative.

Most of these chemical require special handling and special disposal. If you find these, or other hazardous materials, **do not just discard or dump these items.** Some may have decomposed to the extent that even moving or opening the stock bottles could present a serious toxicity or explosion hazard. Consult with professional hazardous waste experts such as those with your state environmental protection agencies. Contract with responsible hazardous waste disposal companies for their removal.

Chemical Name	Chemical Formula	Possible Appearance	Outdated Use	Hazard—Comments
Ammonium dichromate	$(NH_4)_2Cr_2O_7$	Red-orange crystals	Demonstration volcanoes	Unstable; produces toxic byproducts when burned
Benedict's solution		Blue liquid	Test for sugar	Caustic; not appropriate below high school level
Biological Stains: Hematoxylin Safranin Methyl orange Methyl red	Various	Strong colors	Slide preparation	Many are dark permanent stains, difficult to remove from skin and clothing; some have been found to be toxic, carcinogenic, or teratogenic (causing malformations in embryos or fetuses of pregnant women); check latest information prior to use
Calcium carbide	CaC_2	Grayish-black lumps	Mixed with water to release acetylene	Fire and explosion hazard
Carbon tetrachloride	CCl_4	Clear, colorless liquid	Organic solvent	Poison by inhalation and skin absorption; carcinogen
Chlordane		Amber-colored liquid	Pesticide	Easily absorbed through skin and mucous membranes; highly toxic; EPA has banned from use
Chloroform	$CHCl_3$	Clear, colorless liquid	Anesthetic	Human inhalation can cause death; EPA lists as carcinogen
Colchinine	$C_{22}H_{25}NO_6$	Liquid	Preparation of mitotic slides	Highly toxic
Concentrated inorganic acids	(e.g., HNO_3, HCl, H_2SO_4, H_3PO_4)	Liquids	Various	Highly corrosive; some are volatile as well; serious burn and eye-damage hazard
Diethyl ether	$C_2H_5OC_2H_5$	Clear liquid (usually in a metal can)	Anesthetizing insects	Forms explosive peroxides slowly on exposure to air
Elemental mercury	Hg	Silver-colored liquid	Thermometers and barometers; illustration of density; electro-motive replacement demos	Highly toxic; absorbed through the skin; vapors readily absorbed via respiratory tract

Chemical Name	Chemical Formula	Possible Appearance	Outdated Use	Hazard—Comments
Elemental potassium	K		Demonstrate elements	Forms explosive oxides slowly on exposure to air
Elemental sodium	Na	Grayish non-uniform lumps	Explosive oxidation	Violent reaction with water releasing concentrated NaOH fumes and spray
Formaldehyde solution (also called formalin)	HCHO	Colorless clear or cloudy liquid	Preservative	Strong skin and mucous membrane irritant; carcinogen
Magnesium strips	Mg	Slim silvery coiled metal	Wicks for demo volcanoes; "sparklers"	Burns at very high temperature releasing UV light that may damage eyes
Mineral talc	$Mg_3Si_4O_{10}(OH)_2$	Soft, white or gray mineral or white powder	Moh scale mineral; demonstration of cratering	May contain asbestos and cause respiratory problems
Picric acid	2,4,6-trinitrophenol	Clear to yellowish liquid	Specimen preservative	Unstable and explosive if allowed to dry to less than 10% water content
Potassium chlorate	$KClO_3$	White crystals	Generation of oxygen	Strong oxidizer that can cause violent reactions
Potassium cyanide be	KCN	White granules or powder	Insect killing jars	Highly toxic; decomposes on exposure to air and moisture to produce deadly hydrogen cyanide gas; can absorbed through skin or mucous membranes
Silver cyanide	AgCN	White or grayish powder	Silver plating; creating mirrored surfaces	Toxic; can be absorbed through skin or mucous membranes
Sodium hydroxide	NaOH	Small milky-colored pellets	Demonstration of exothermic reactions and acid/base experiments	Highly caustic; serious permanent eye-damage hazard from splash and fumes released during reactions
White phosphorous	P	White or yellowish waxy-looking sticks stored in water	Demonstrate spontaneous combustion	Spontaneous combustion; fire that is very difficult to extinguish; small particles remaining continue to reignite

Appendix B

NSTA Position Statement on Safety

Safety and School Science Instruction

Preamble

Inherent in many instructional settings including science is the potential for injury and possible litigation. These issues can be avoided or reduced by the proper application of a safety plan.

Rationale

High quality science instruction includes laboratory investigations, interactive or demonstration activities and field trips.

Declarations

The National Science Teachers Association recommends that school districts and teachers adhere to the following guidelines:

▶ School districts must adopt written safety standards, hazardous material management and disposal procedures for chemical and biological wastes. These procedures must meet or exceed the standards adopted by EPA, OSHA and/or appropriate state and local agencies.

▶ School authorities and teachers share the responsibility of establishing and maintaining safety standards.

▶ School authorities are responsible for providing safety equipment (i.e., fire extinguishers), personal protective equipment (i.e., eye wash stations, goggles), Material Safety Data Sheets and training appropriate for each science teaching situation.

▶ School authorities will inform teachers of the nature and limits of liability and tort insurance held by the school district.

- All science teachers must be involved in an established and on-going safety training program relative to the established safety procedures which is updated on an annual basis.

- Teachers shall be notified of individual student heath concerns.

- The maximum number of occupants in a laboratory teaching space shall be based on the following:

  1. the building and fire safety codes;

  2. occupancy load limits;

  3. design of the laboratory teaching facility;

  4. appropriate supervision and the special needs of students.

- Materials intended for human consumption shall not be permitted in any space used for hazardous chemicals and or materials.

- Students and parents will receive written notice of appropriate safety regulations to be followed in science instructional settings.

References

Section 1008.0 Occupant Load — BOAC National Building Code/1996

Section 10-1.7.0 Occupant Load — NFPA Life Safety Code 101-97

40 CFR 260-70 Resource Conservation and Recovery Act (RCRA)

29 CFR 1910.1200 Hazard Communication Standard (Right to Know Law)

29 CFR 1910.1450 Laboratory Standard , Part Q The Laboratory Standard (Chemical Hygiene Law)

National Research Council (1995). *Prudent Practices in the Laboratory*, National Academy Press.

Furr, K. Ed. (1995). *Handbook of Laboratory Safety*, 4th Ed. CRC Press.

Fleming, et al Eds. (1995). *Laboratory Safety*, 2nd Ed. ASM Press.

National Science Education Leadership Position Paper. (1997). Class size in laboratory rooms. *The Navigator.* 33(2).

Authors

George R. Hague, Jr., Chair, Science Safety Advisory Board, St. Mark's School of Texas, Dallas, TX 75230

Douglas Mandt, Immediate Past-Chair, Science Safety Advisory Board, Science Education Consultant, Edgewood, WA 98372

Dennis D. Bromley, Safety Instructor, Independent Contractor, Anchorage, AK 99502

Donna M. Brown, Radnor Township School District, Wayne, PA 19087

Frances S. Hess, Cooperstown H.S., Cooperstown, NY 13326

Lorraine Jones, Kirby H.S., Nashville, TN

William F. McComas, Director, NSTA District XVI, University of Southern California, Los Angeles, CA 90089

Kenneth Roy, Glastonbury Public Schools, Glastonbury, CT 06033

Linda D. Sinclair, South Carolina Department of Education, Columbia, SC 29201

Colette Skinner, Henderson, NV 89015

Olivia C. Swinton, Patricia Roberts Harris, Education Center, Washington, D.C.
Nina Visconti-Phillips, Assistance & Resources Integrating Science Education (ARISE) Dayton, NJ 08810

—Adopted by the NSTA Board of Directors, July 2000

Appendix C

American Chemical Society Safety Guidelines

Chemical Safety for Teachers and Their Supervisors: Grades 7-12

The full text of the American Chemical Society's 32-page safety guide for grades 7-12 is available at *membership.acs.org/c/ccs/pubs/chemical_safety_manual.pdf*

Teachers can order single copies on request. For information, call ACS at 800-227-5558, e-mail oss@acs.org, or write Office of Society Services, American Chemical Society, 1155 16th Street, NW, Washington, DC 20036.

In the first section, "Safety in the Use and Handling of Hazardous Chemical," the topics are Labels and Material Safety Data Sheets, Chemical Hazards, Eye Protection, Flammability, Corrosivity, Toxicity, Reactivity, and Physical Hazards.

In the second section, "Teaching Safety to Our Students and Other Safety Considerations," the topics are Risks versus Benefits, Accident/Incident Records, Insidious Hazards, and Safety Inspections.

In the third section, "Preparing Your Own Safety Checklist," the topics are Work Habits, Safety Wear, Facilities and Equipment, Purchase, Use, and Disposal of Chemicals, and Substitutions.

The fourth section is "A Commentary on Safety."

The guide also includes an introduction, a section for supervisors on how to use the guide, references, acknowledgements, and an index.

Index

Index

Index

Index

Index

Index

Index

Index